The Worlds Animals:

From A to Z with Color and

Rhyme!

Kevin Ernst

DEDICATION

This book is dedicated to my wife Sarah,
who lets me chase hairbrained ideas while watching me
get distracted by shiny things.

ACKNOWLEDGMENTS

I want to thank my wife and kids and grandkids for never looking at me and asking what the hell I was doing. They just always went with the flow.

Thank You:

Kailey, Charlie, Sara, Lorryn
Lyla and Tiny Toes

A is for Antelope

On Africa's vast savannas, the antelope run and play,

With curved horns and nimble legs, they brighten up the day.

They graze on Africa's grasses, filling their tummies with glee,

And when danger lurks nearby, their speed sets them free!

Some antelopes are tiny, while others reach great height,

But one thing they have in common: they run with great might.

Antelopes come in different shapes, sizes, and hues,

And with their graceful movements, they're creatures that will amuse!

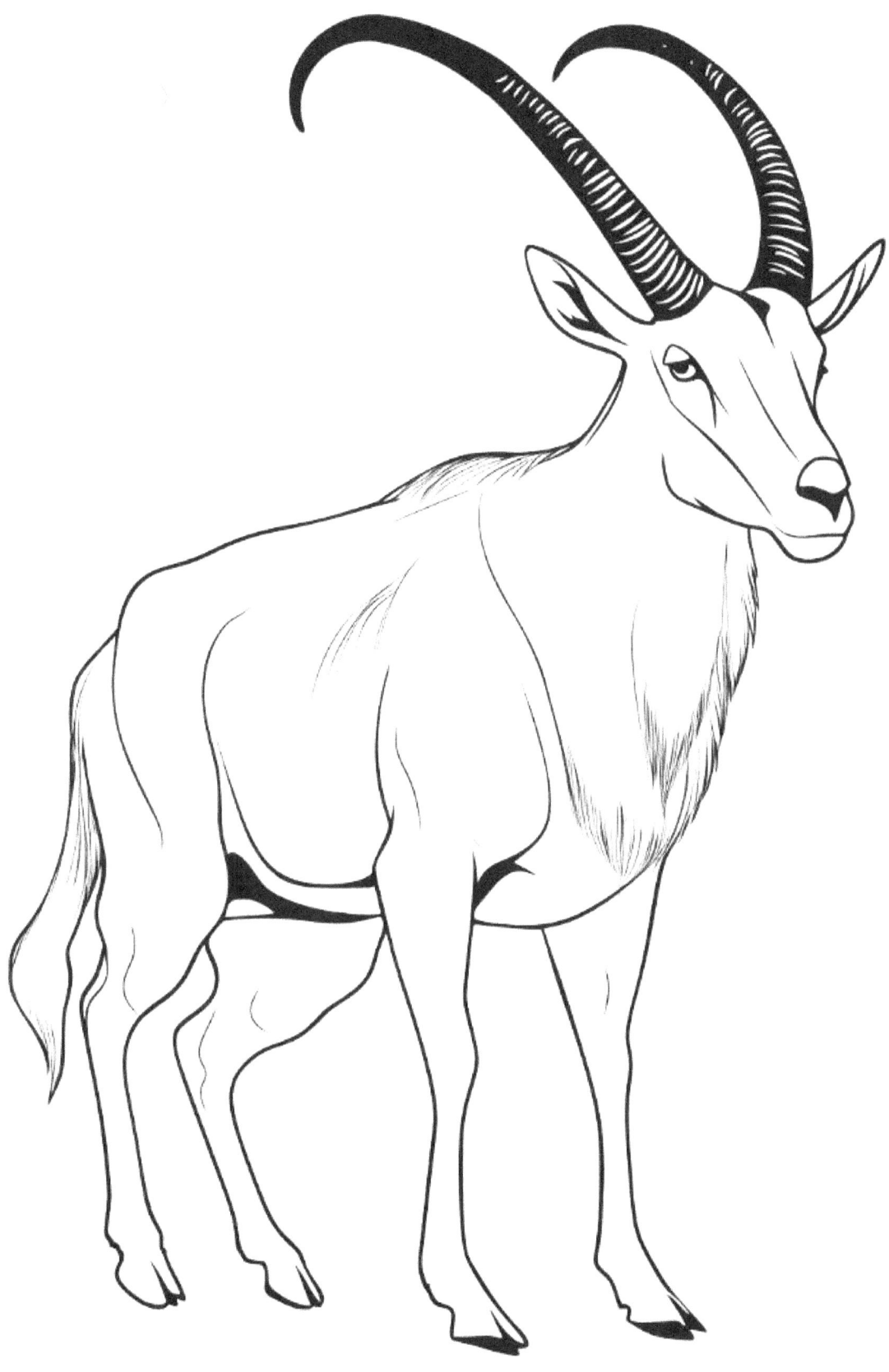

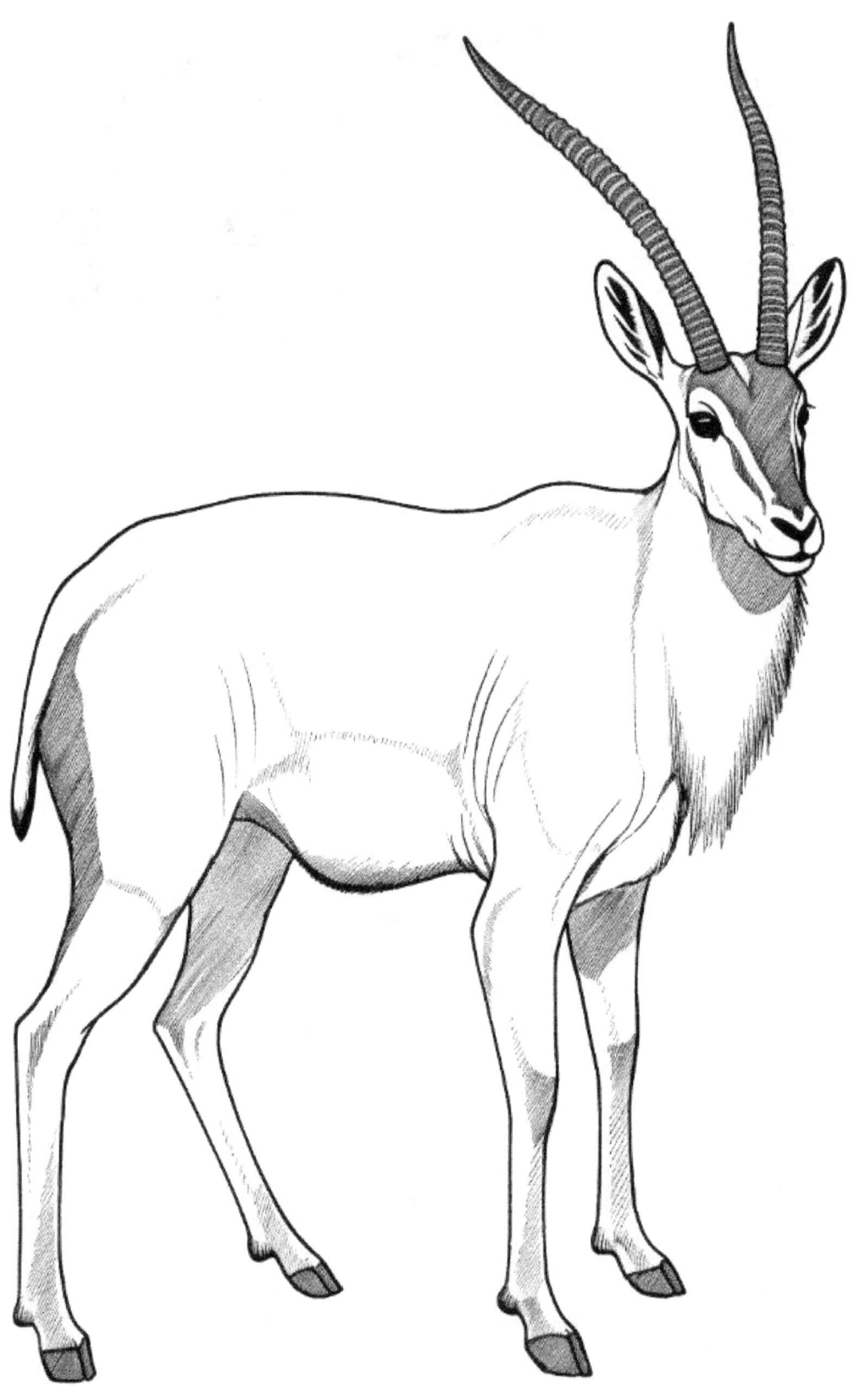

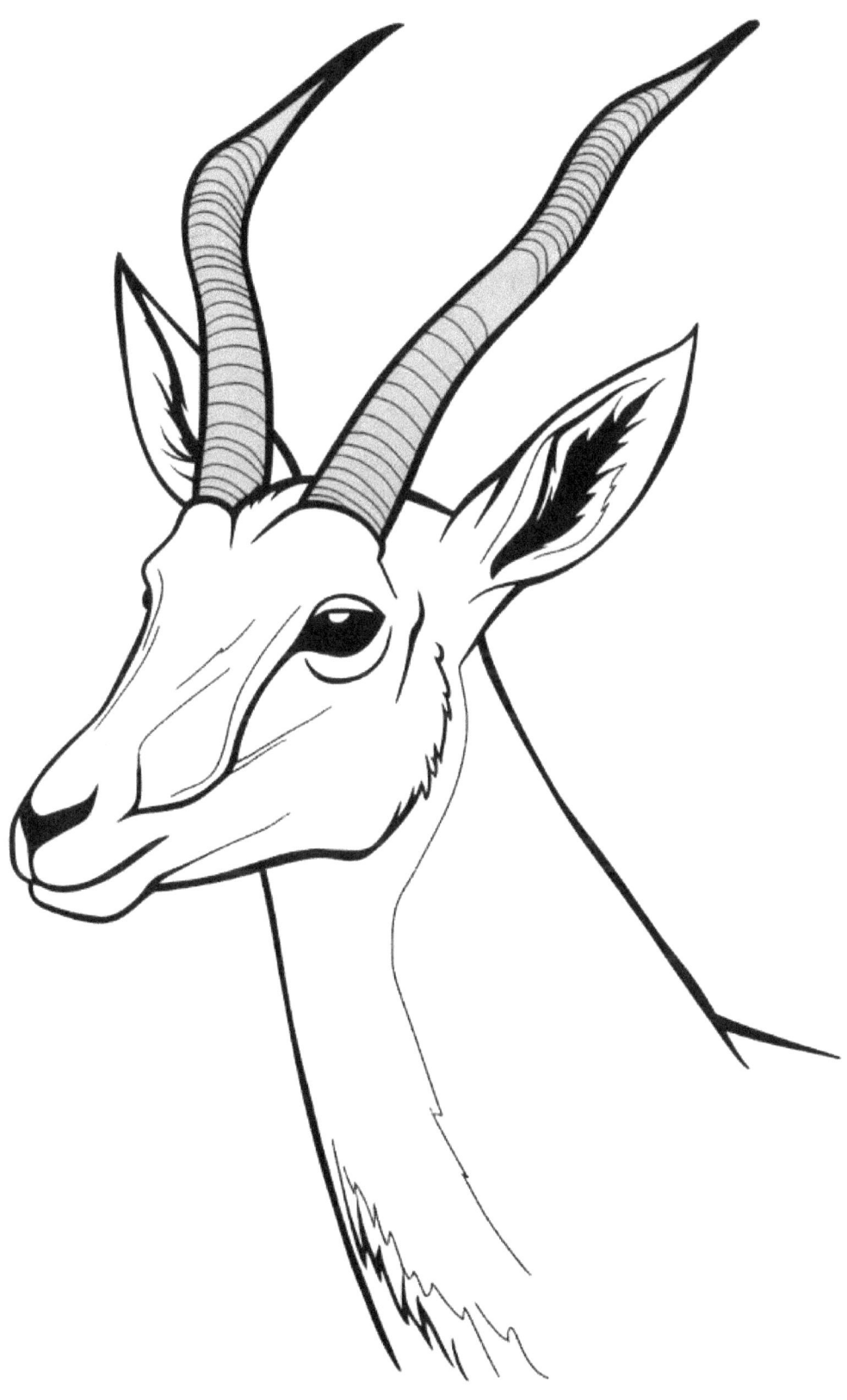

B is for Bear

In the forest deep and dark, the bear roams free,

A fierce and mighty creature, with strength all can see.

With thick fur and claws, they're well-equipped to survive,

And in the winter, they hibernate, in a den they will thrive.

Black, white, or brown, they're found all around the world,

And while they may seem cuddly, please leave them alone where they're curled.

They survey the forest at all times, just looking for some delectable eats,

A bear is an awesome sight, a true ruler, one of the forest's elites.

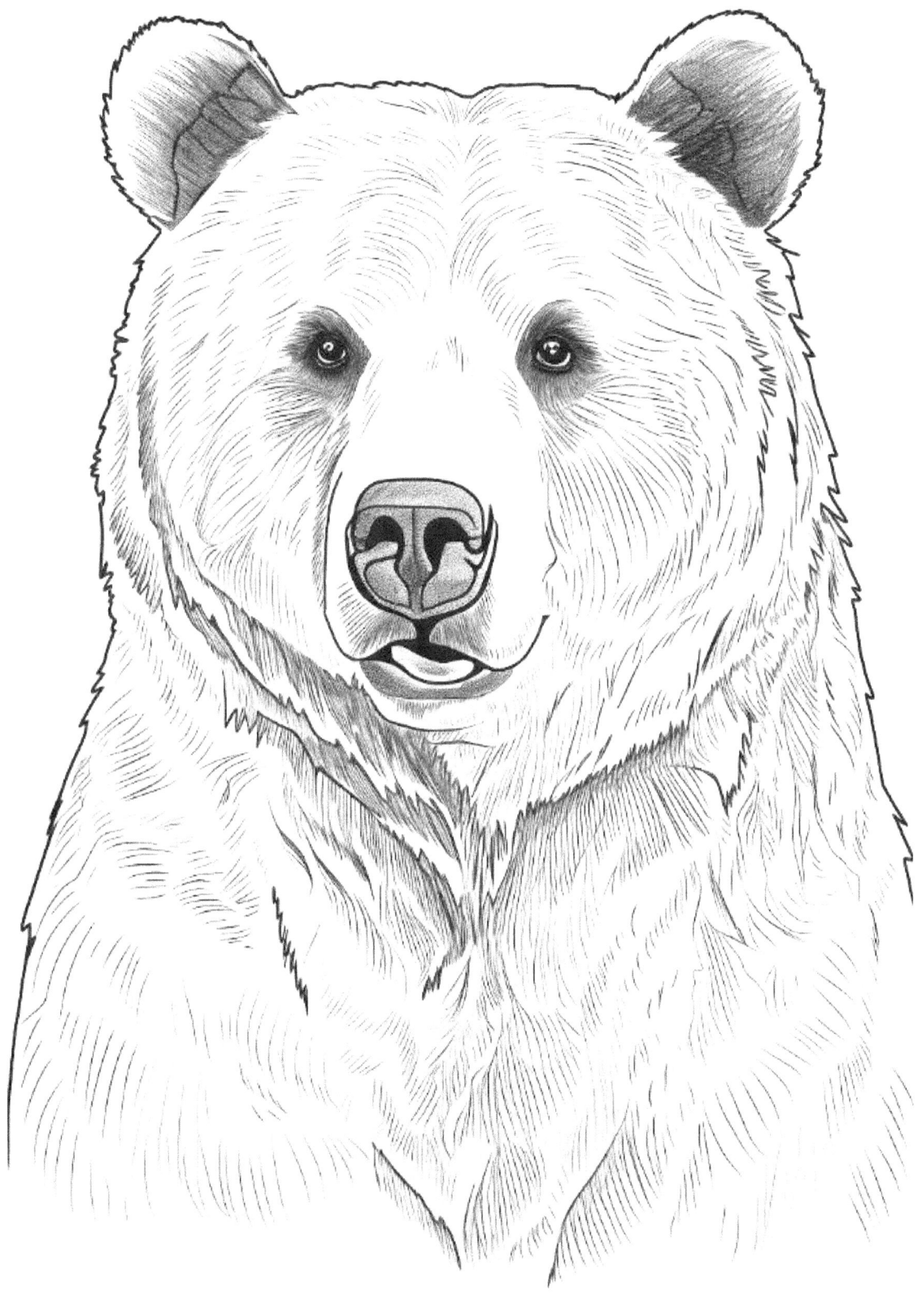

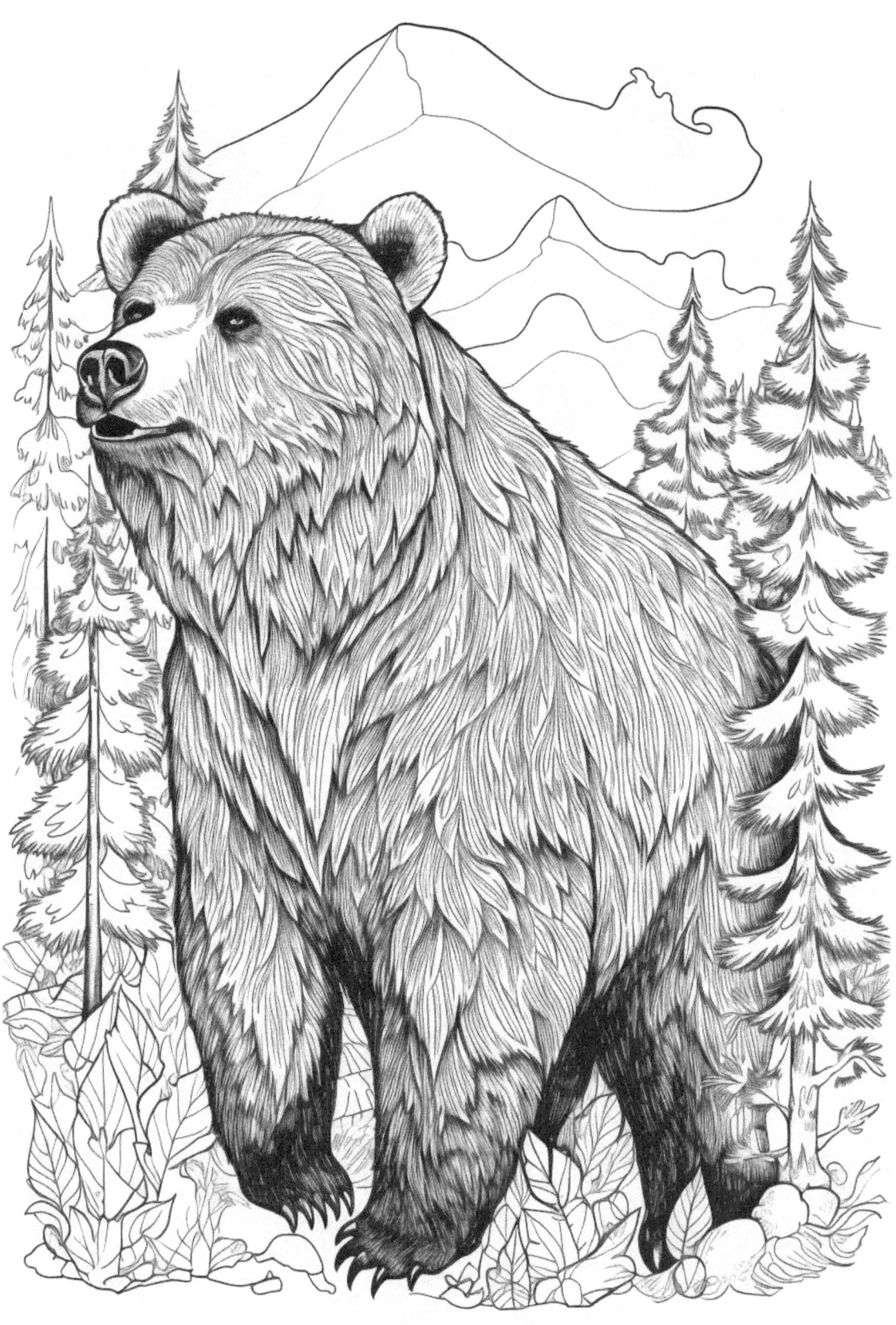

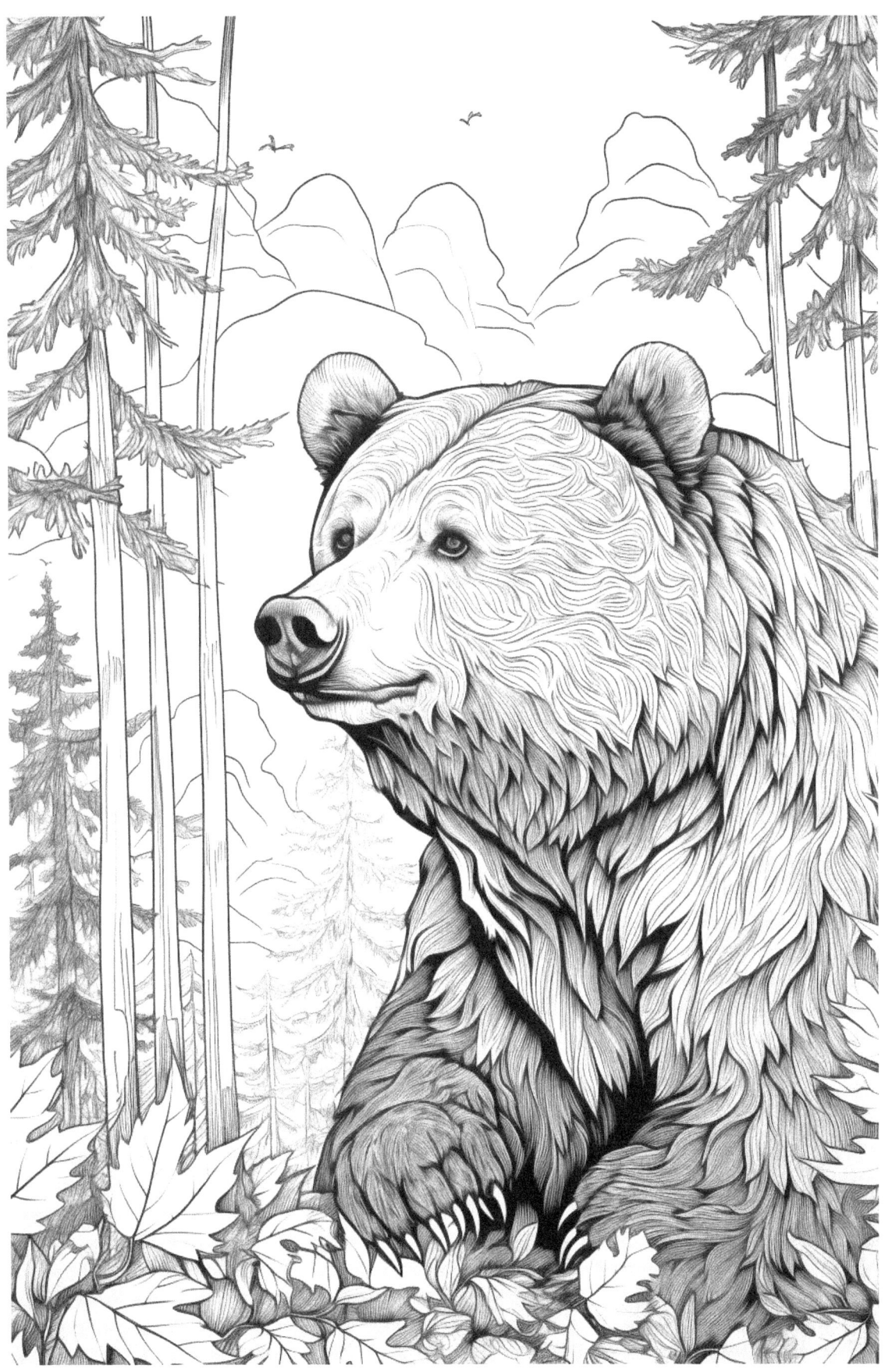

C is for Camel

In the desert's scorching heat, the camel makes its home,

With humps that store fat, fat and water, they can certainly roam.

Camels are gentle creatures, despite their tough exterior shell,

And with their natural ability to carry heavy loads, they help move supplies real swell.

Camels are hardy, resilient, and able to go for days without a drink,

And with their padded feet, they can walk on loose sand and not sink!

They're stand tall and are proud, with long legs to made to stride,

And their thick coat protects them, they don't need to hide.

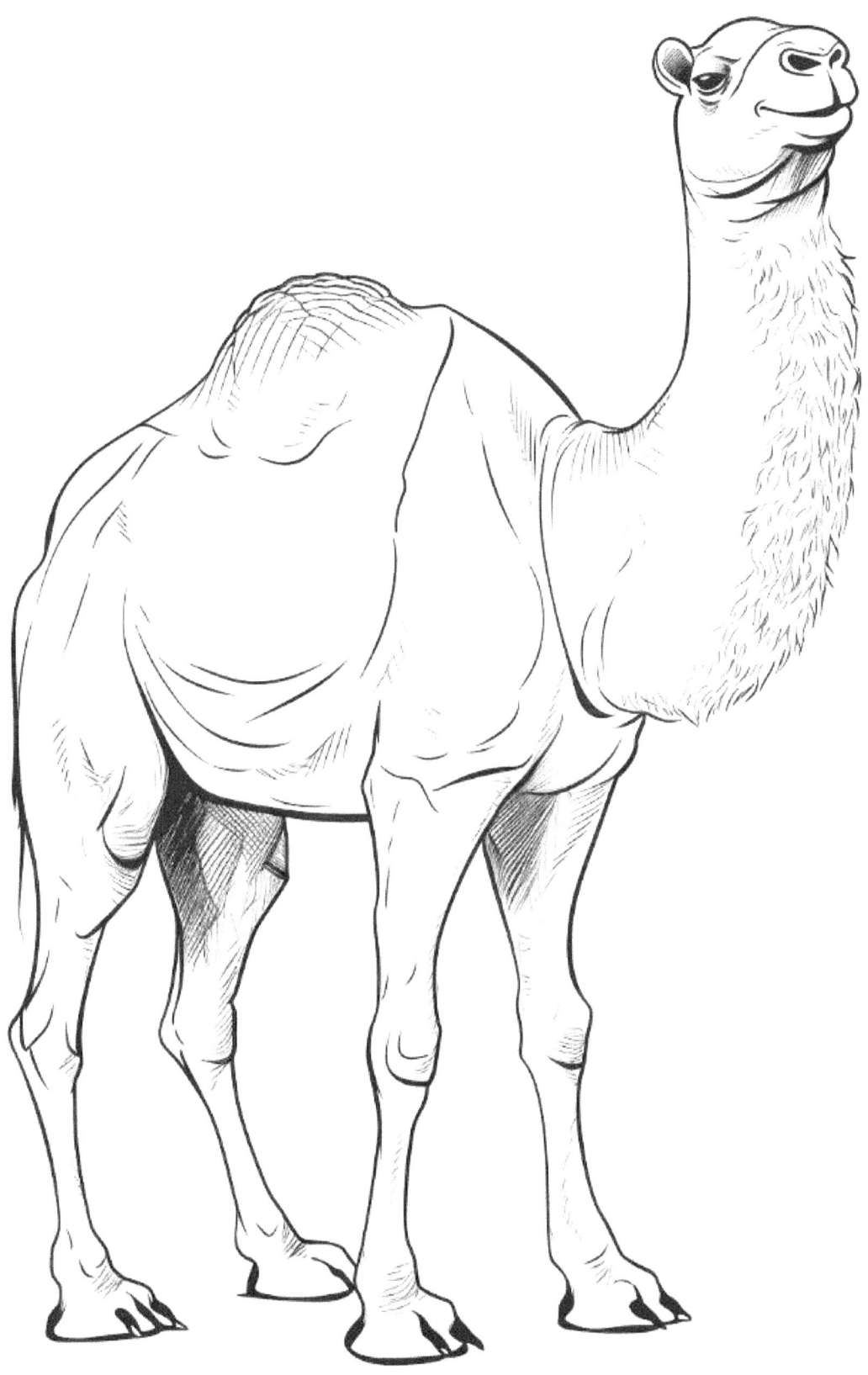

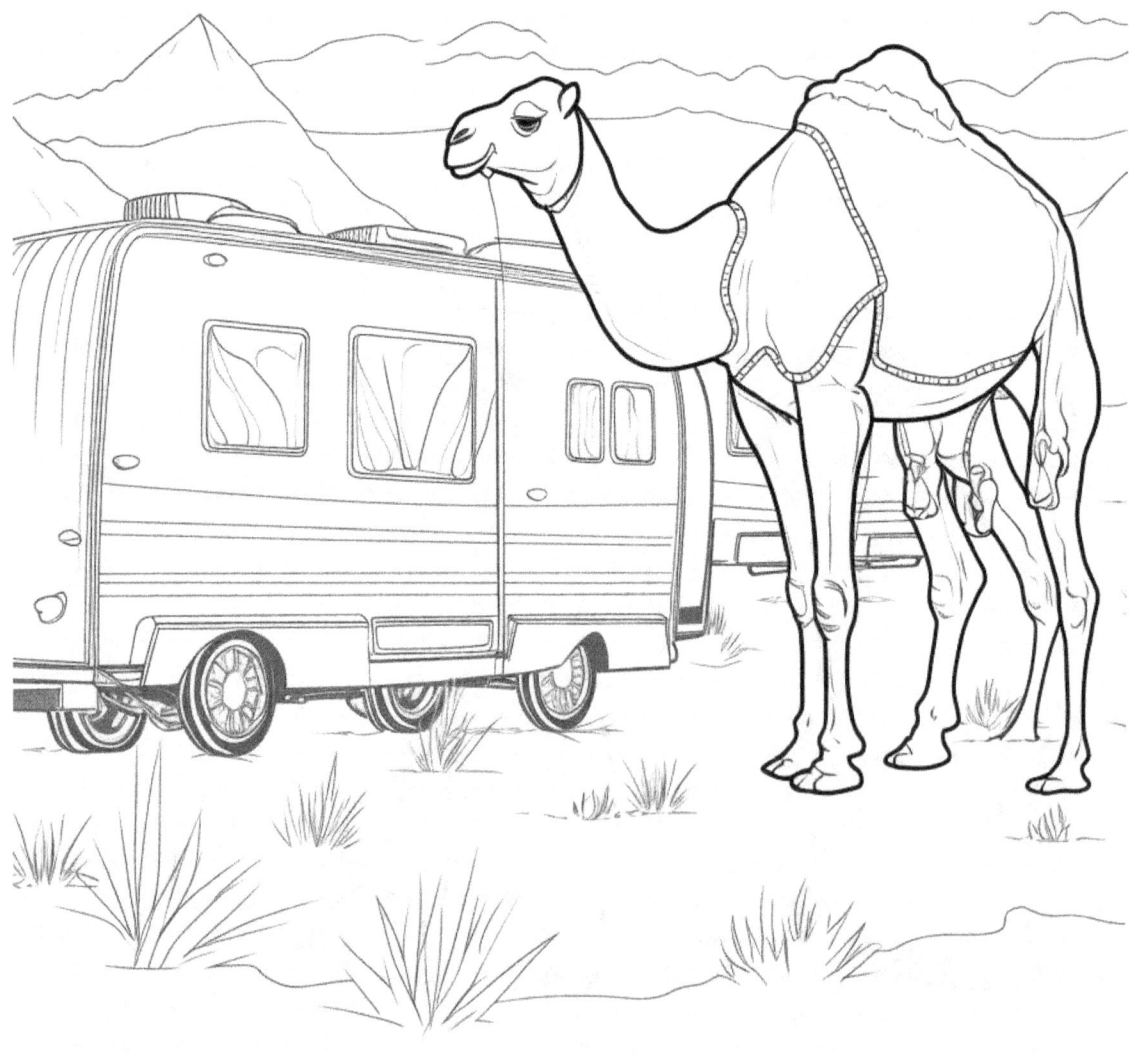

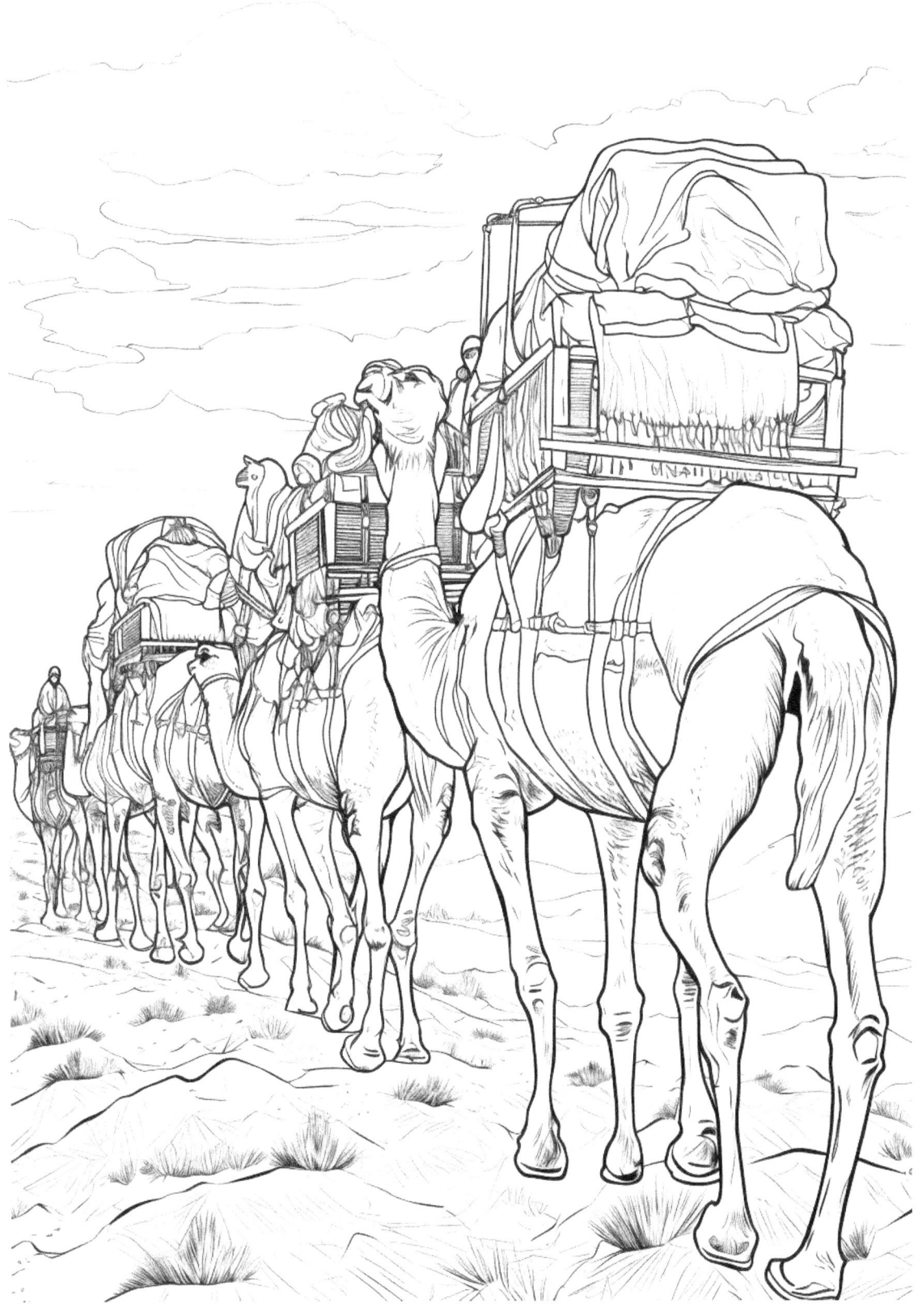

D is for Dolphin

In the ocean deep and wide the dolphin loves to play and dive,

With sleek and agile bodies, they're built for speed and underwater glides.

They communicate with clicks and whistles, a language all their own,

And in pods, they swim and hunt together, a social group they've grown.

From the bottlenose to the spinner, dolphins come in many types,

And with their intelligence and charm, they've won many hearts and likes.

Dolphins breathe air through blowholes on top, and then back into the waves they go,

A dolphin is a sight to see, a creature of grace and flow.

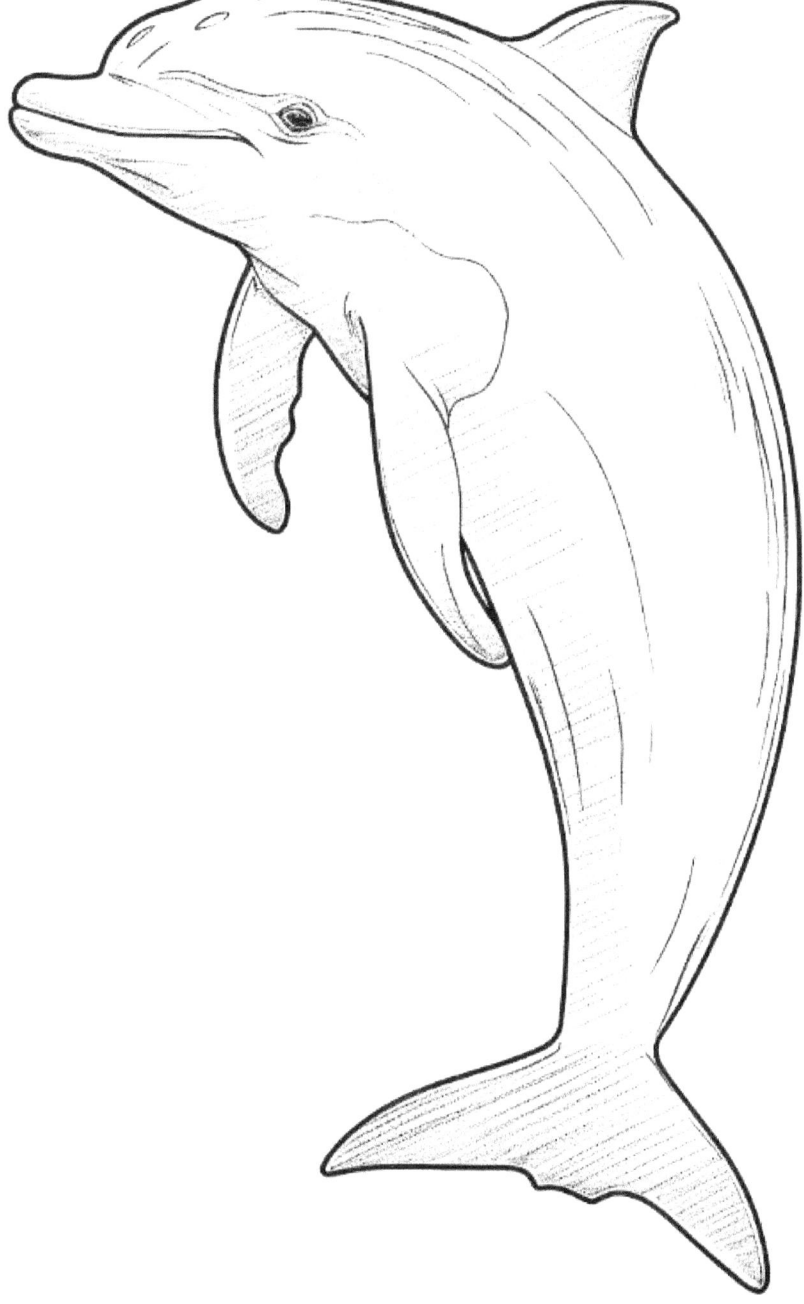

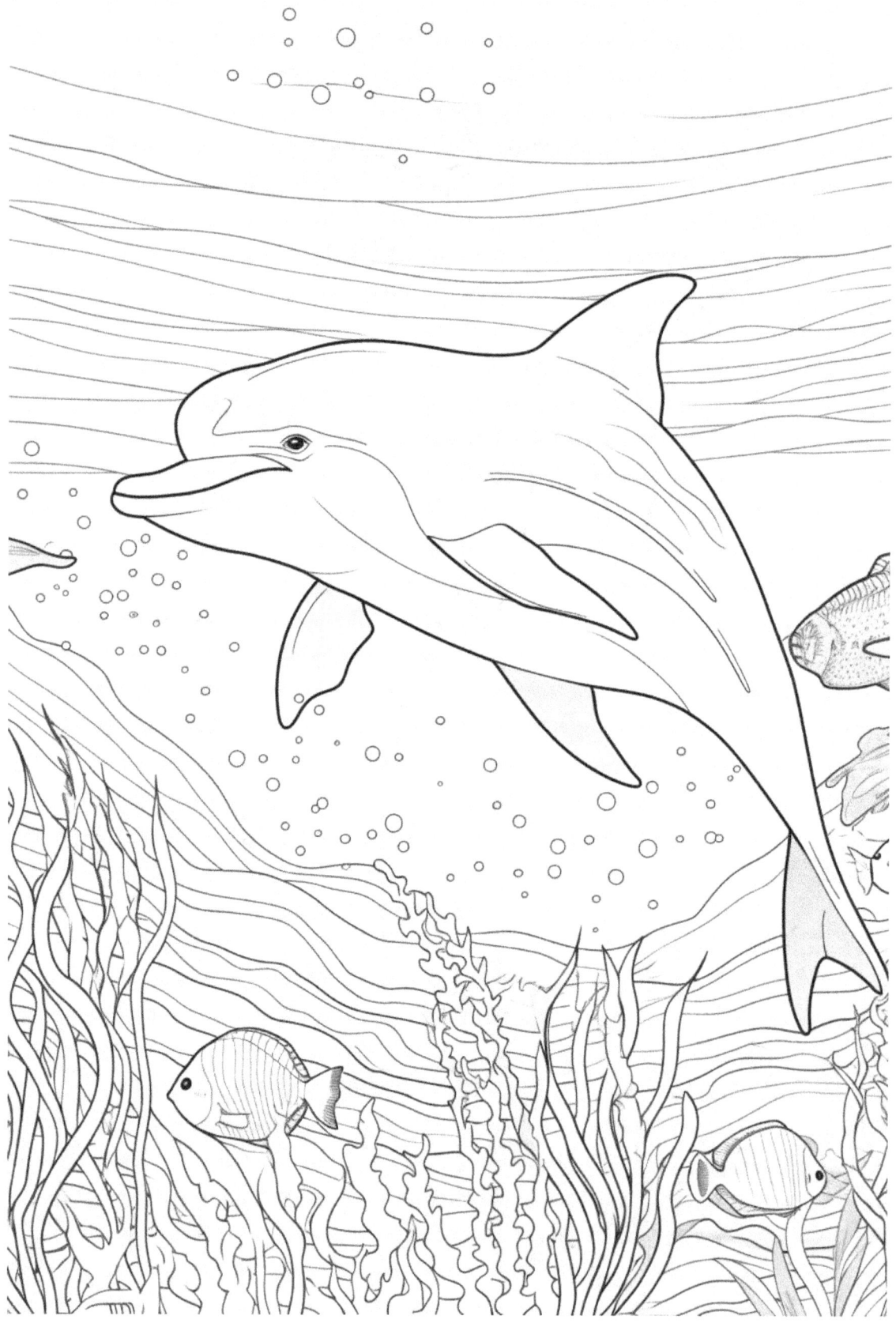

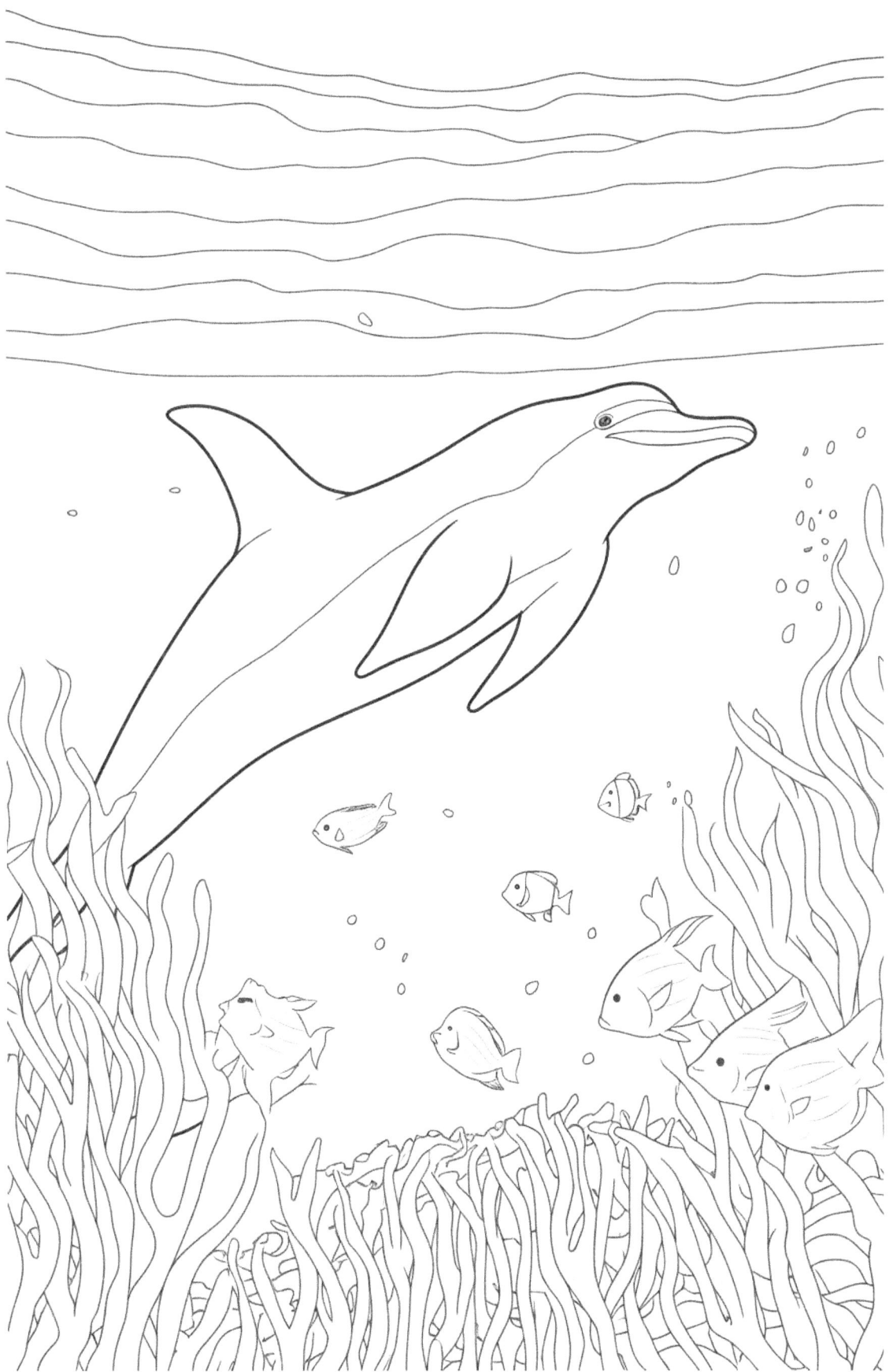

E is for Elephant

In Africa and Asia, the elephant roams and climbs slow like molasses,

With trunks like a hand, they can grab and move around great masses.

Their ears are large and flappy, to help them cool down in the heat,

And with their long tusks, they can dig up roots they can eat.

Elephants are social animals, who live in families that are tight,

And with their intelligence and memory, they're known to be quite bright.

But with poaching and habitat loss, their numbers have declined,

An elephant is a majestic creature, one that people have enshrined.

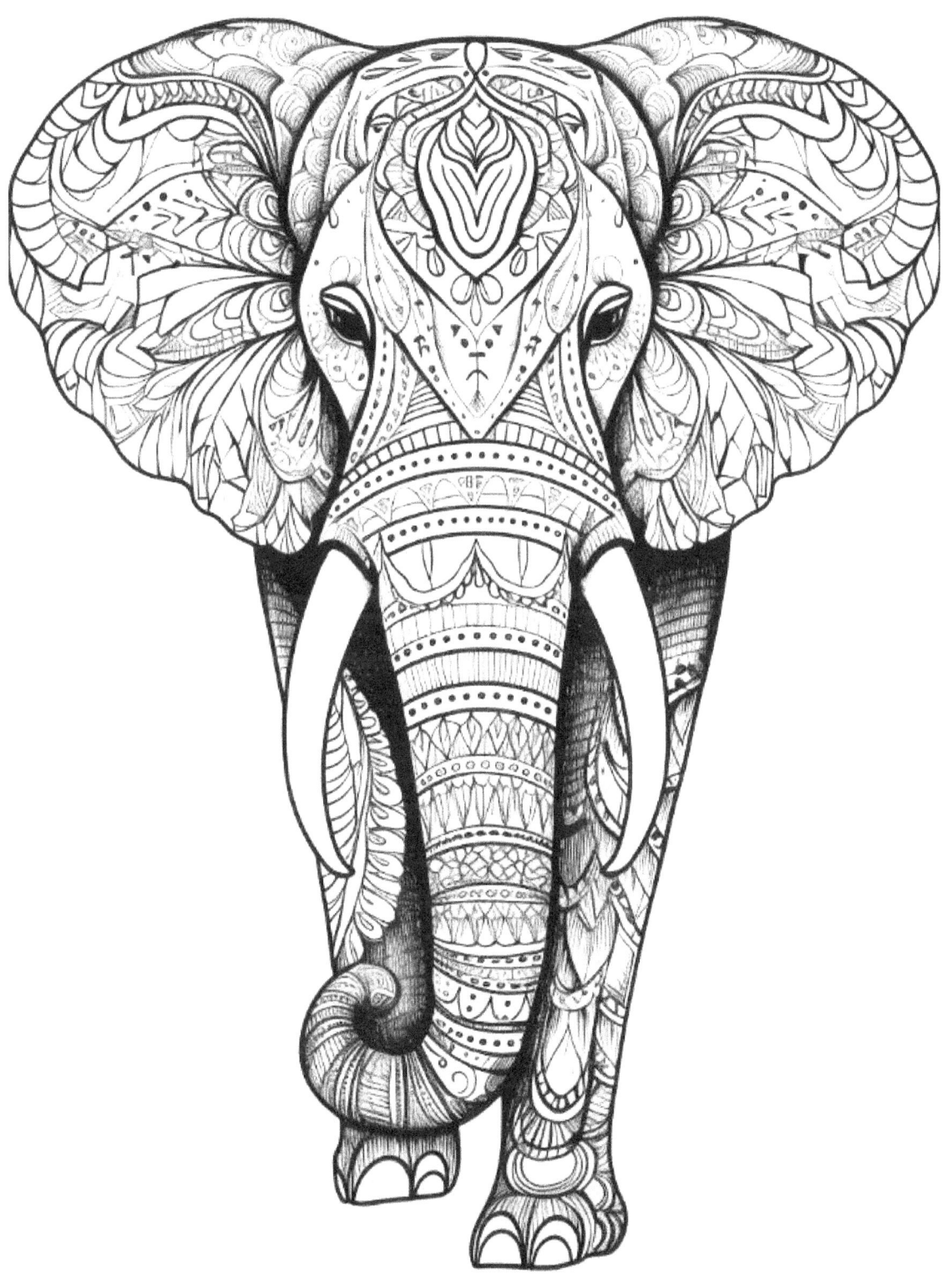

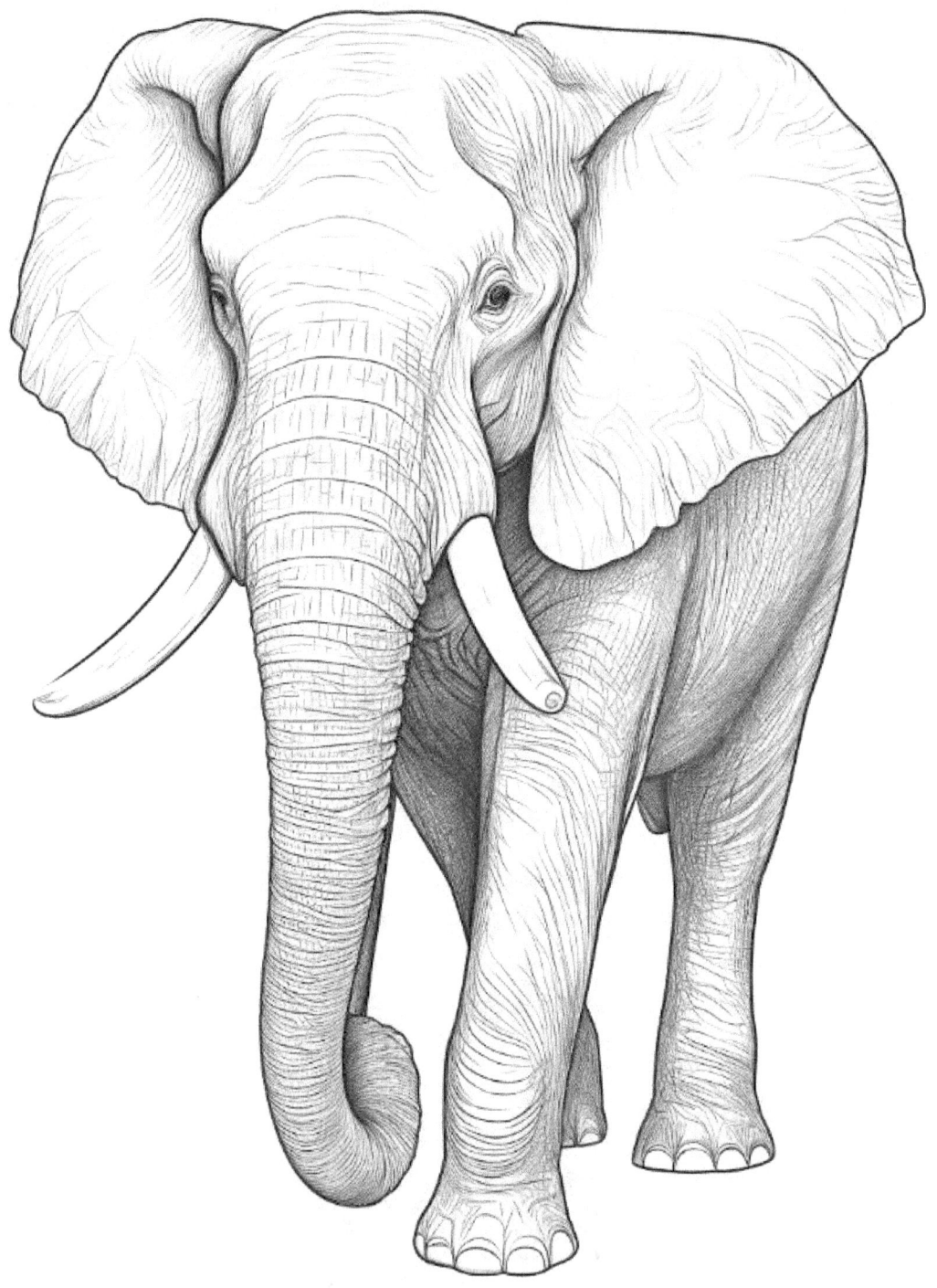

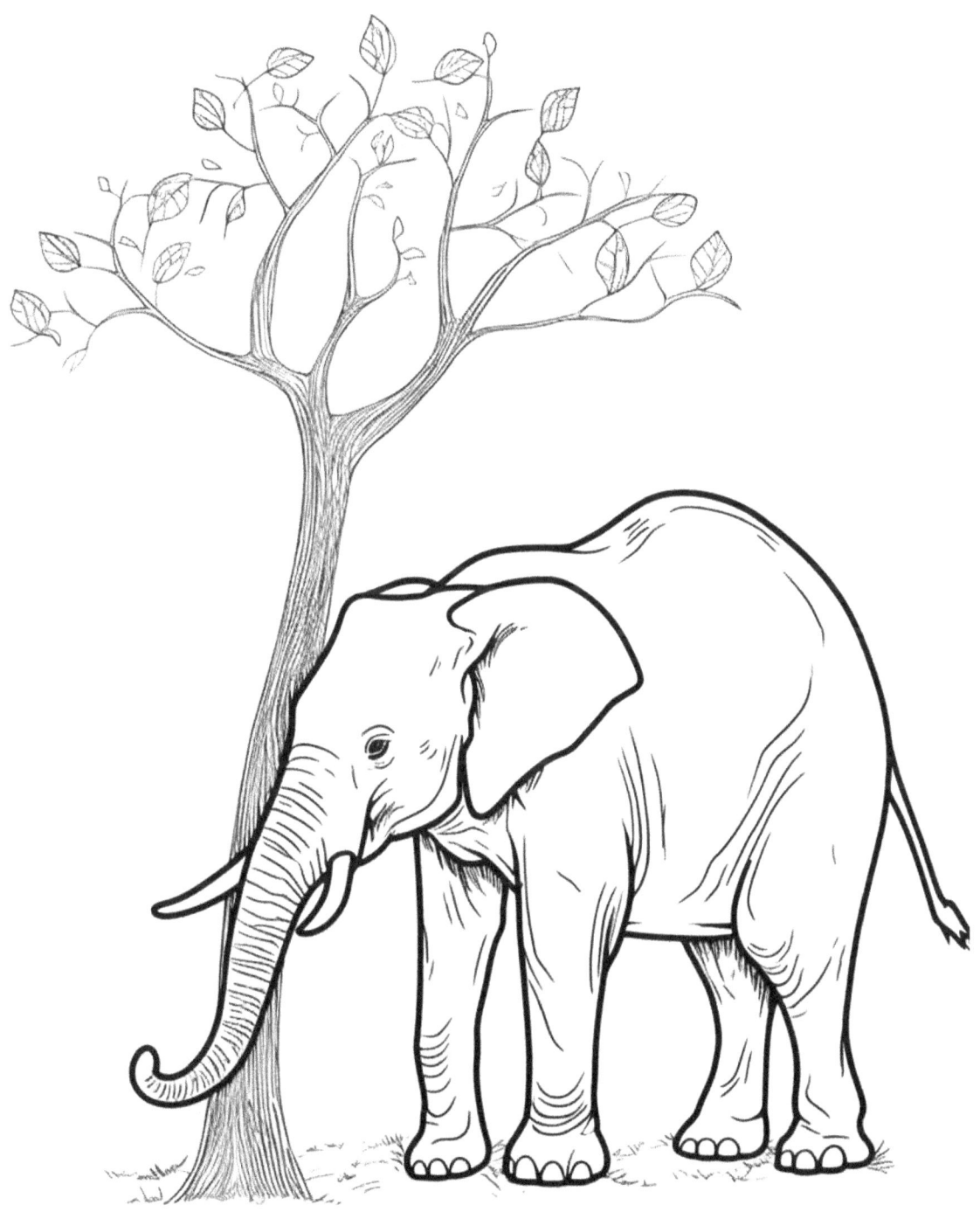

F is for Flamingo

In lagoons and lakes, the flamingo stands tall when it feeds,

With feathers of dyed pink and red, they're quite the colorful amongst reeds.

They feed on shrimp and plankton, by filtering them through their bill,

Standing gracefully with long legs and long necks, a sight that will thrill.

Flamingos often flock together, in groups that can be large,

And with their synchronized movements, they're a visual barrage.

South America, the Caribbean, and Africa, are where they call home I've been told,

A flamingo is a wondrous sight, one that you want to behold!

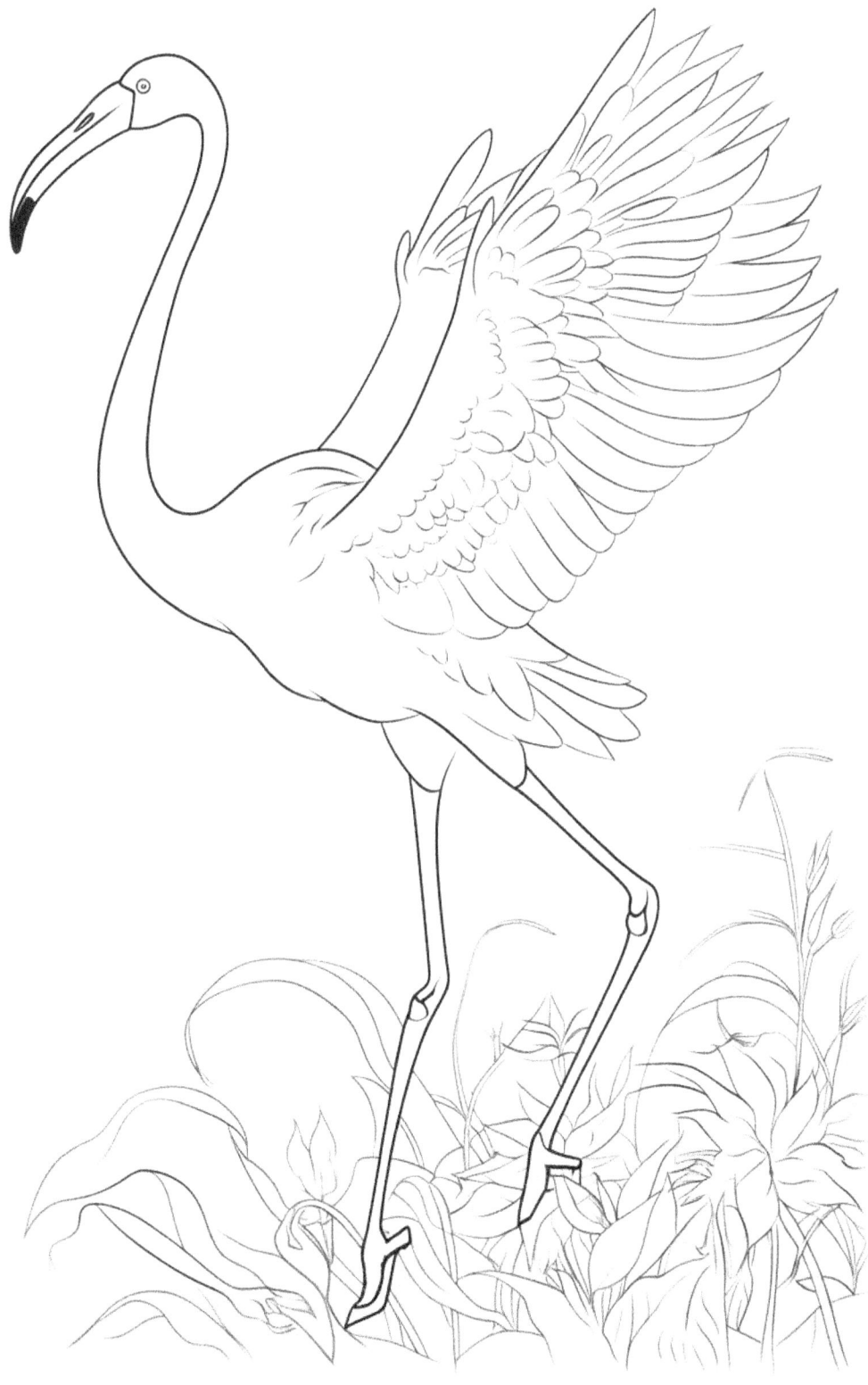

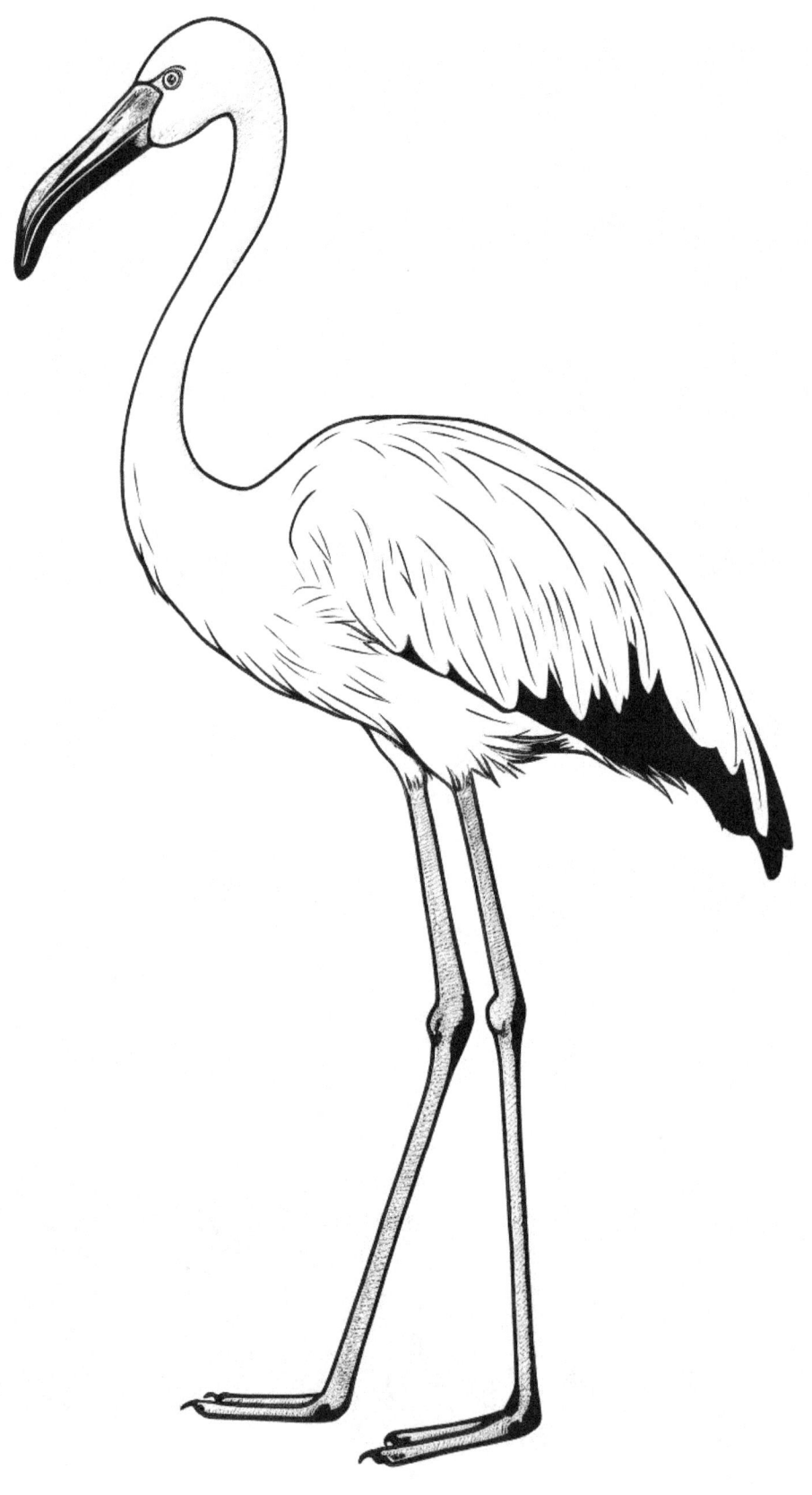

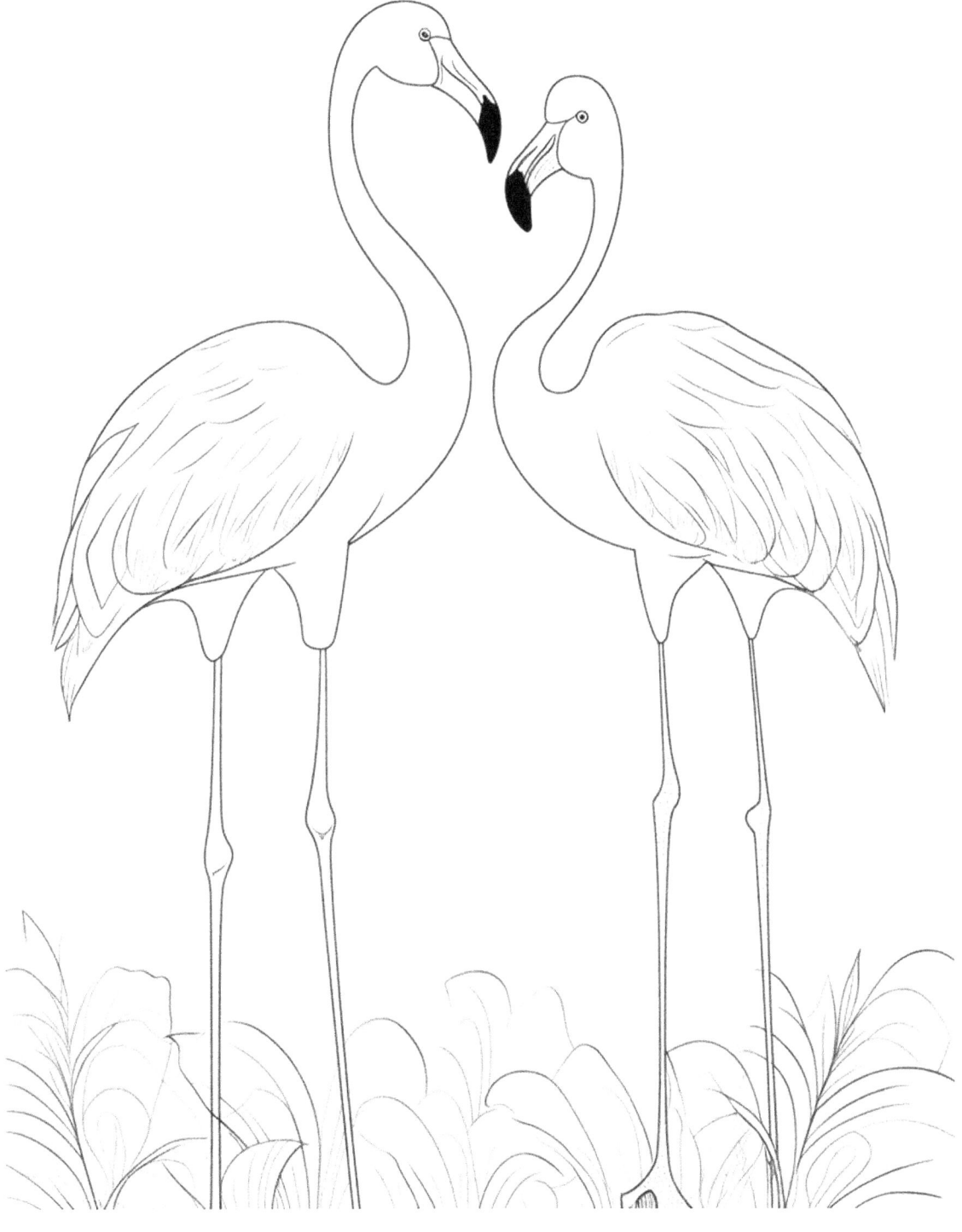

G is for Gopher

A gopher is a critter that tunnels just under the ground,

With strong claws for digging, their large homes are profound.

They snack on roots and bulbs, and sometimes even fruit,

And their underground burrows make soil healthier, to that there's no dispute.

Gophers may be solitary and mostly seen a lone, but they're still a lively sight,

Their playful antics above ground are sure to bring you delight.

So, let's celebrate the gopher, and all the joy that they bring,

Their tunneling and foraging are exceptionally fascinating things!

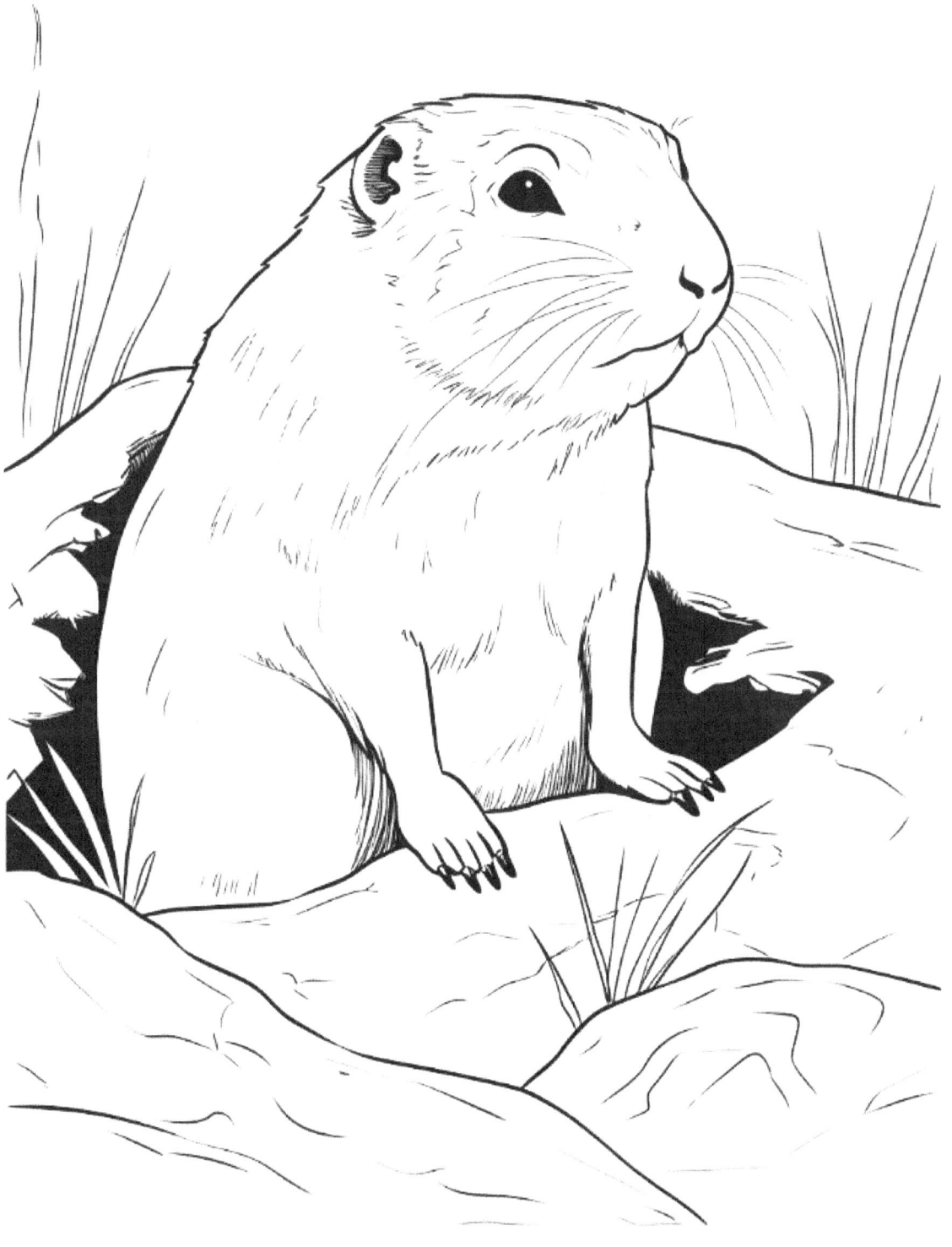

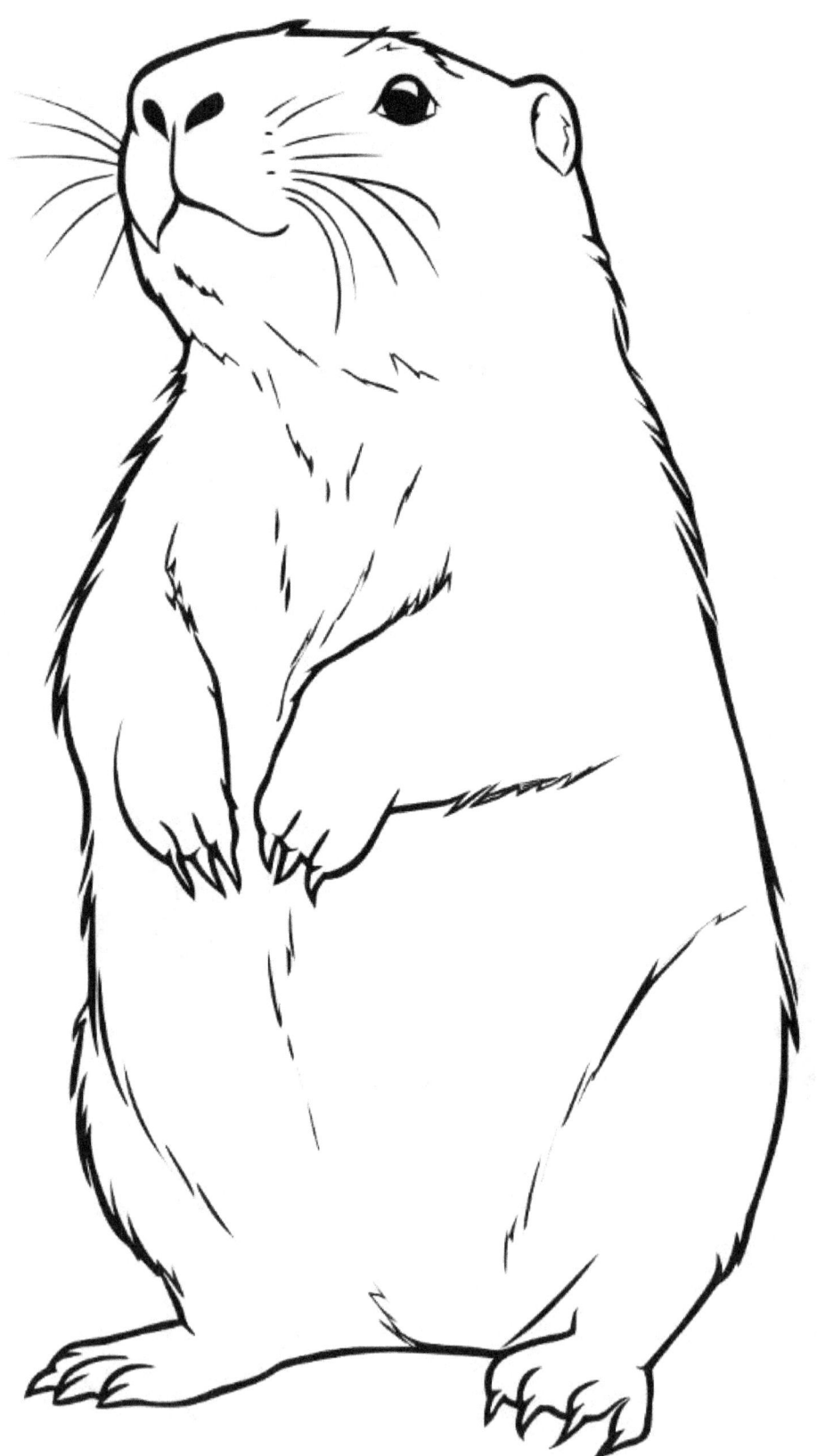

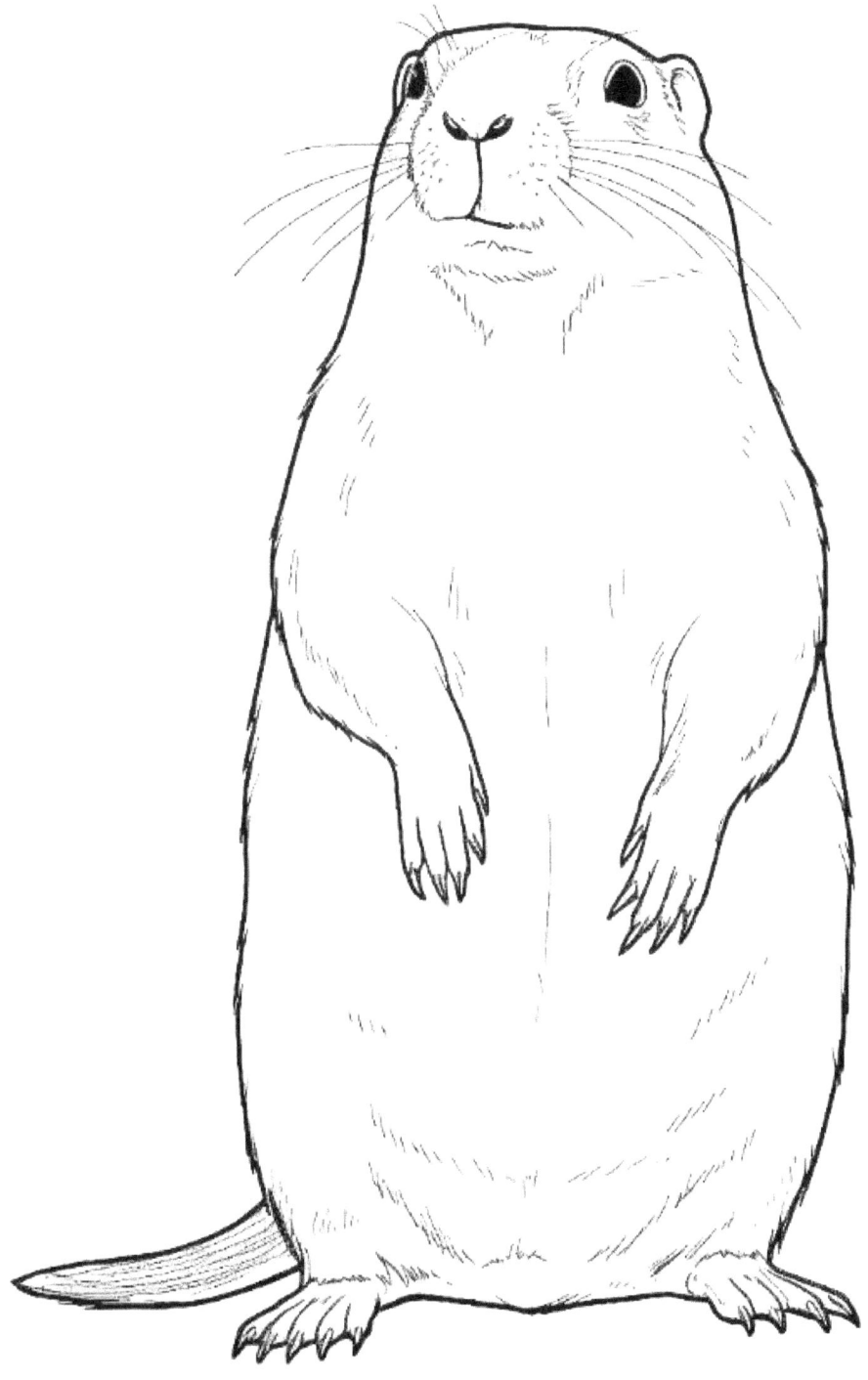

H is for Hippopotamus

In the rivers and lakes of Africa, the hippo spends most its days,

With thick skin and massive size, they're built for the deep waterways.

They graze on land at night, with a diet that's mostly from grass,

And with their sharp teeth and jaws, their defenses are hard to surpass!

Hippos are social creatures, living in groups that can be quite large,

And with their territorial behavior, they guard their space with an angry charge!

With their huge size, strength and speed, they should be elated,

Because a hippo is a creature that's not to be underestimated.

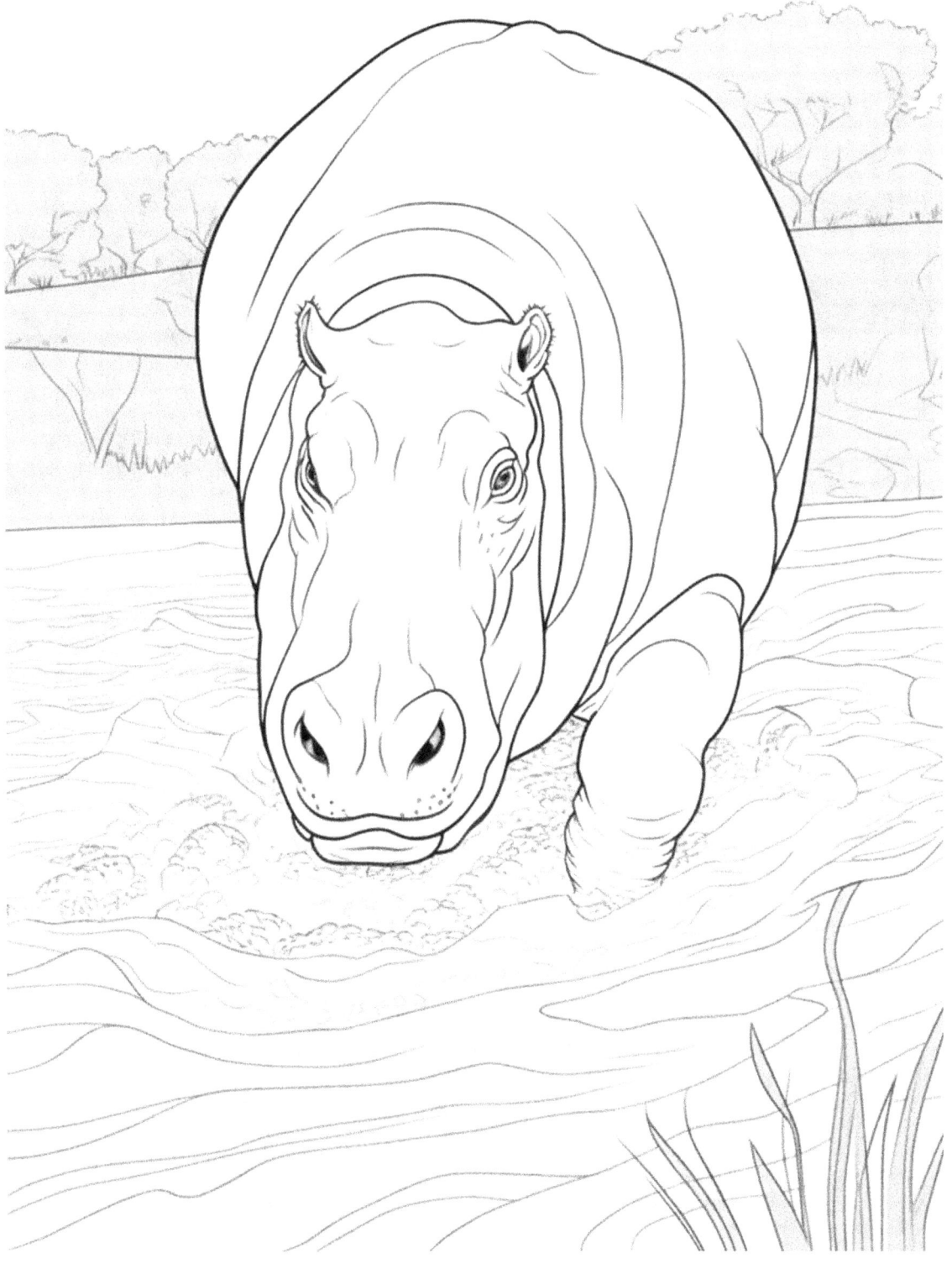

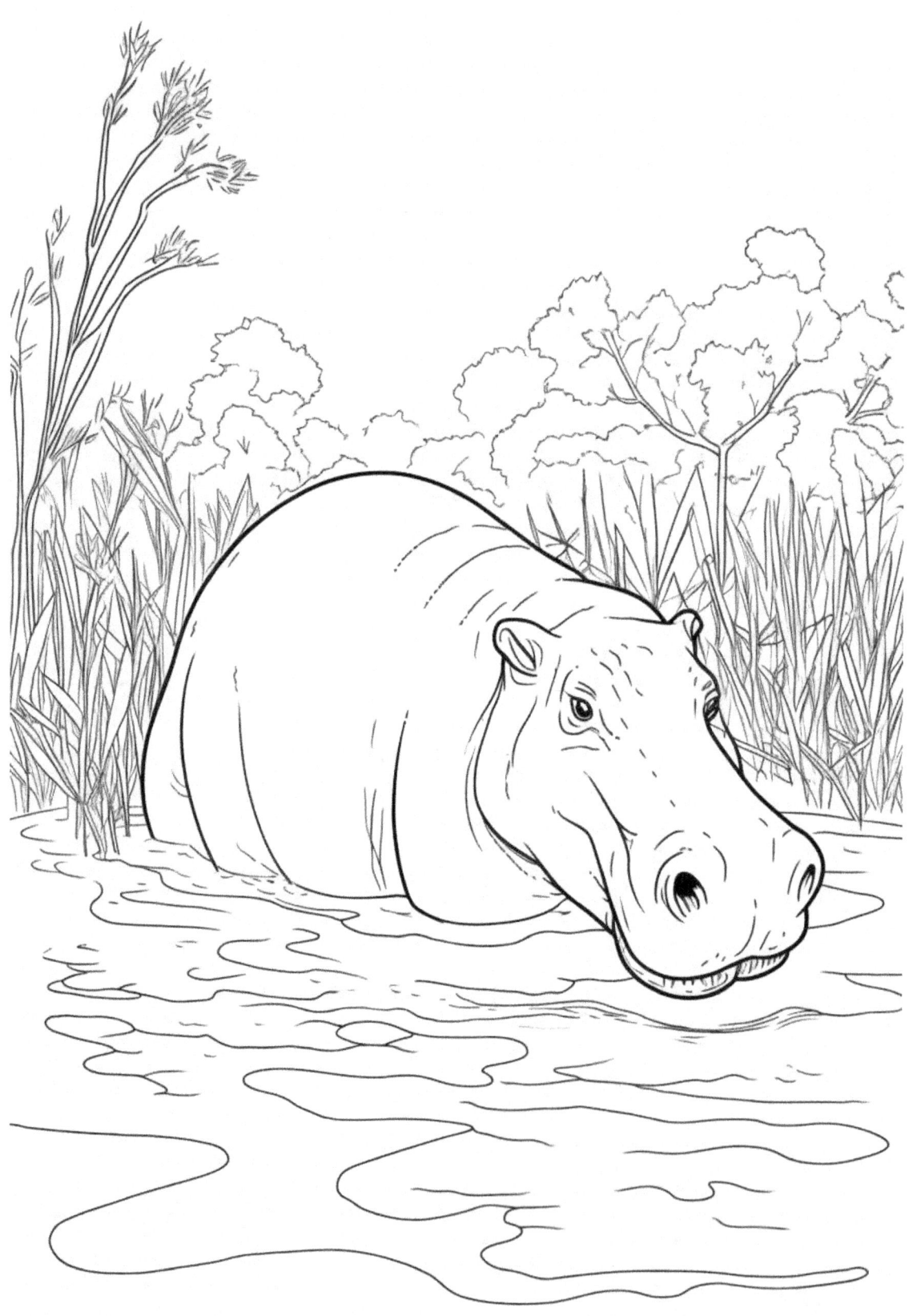

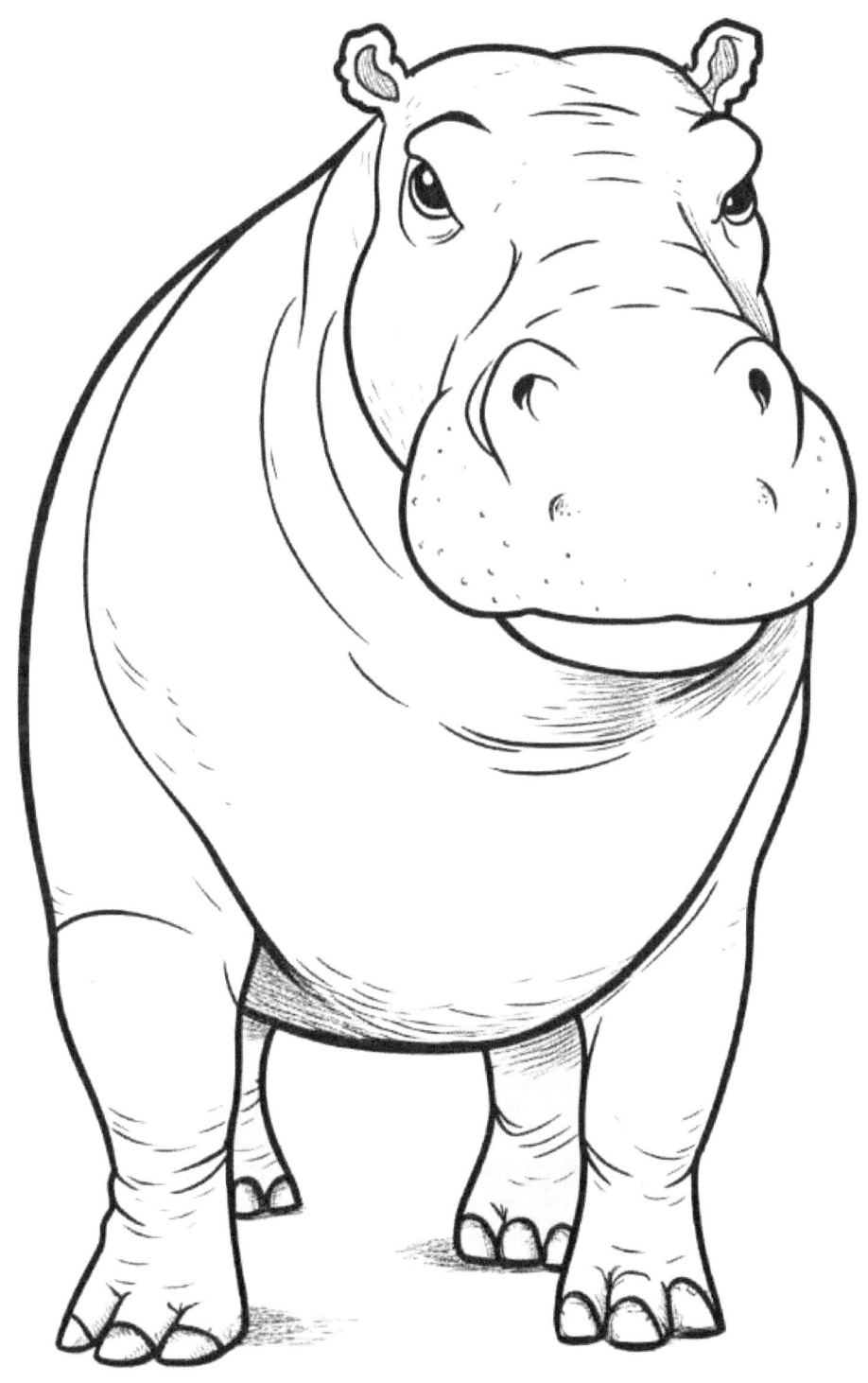

I is for Iguana

In the tropical regions of the Americas, the iguana sunbathes as it climbs,

With scaly skin and sharp claws, they're creatures that stood the test of time.

They're herbivores that eat leaves and fruits, and occasionally insects too,

And with their sharp vision and hearing, they can detect threats and pursue.

Iguanas have a unique defense, using their tails to strike fast as a whip,

And with their ability to change color, they can blend in and hide on a surface and grip.

With protection from predators, their populations can rise,

An iguana is a wondrous creature, one that will definitely surprise.

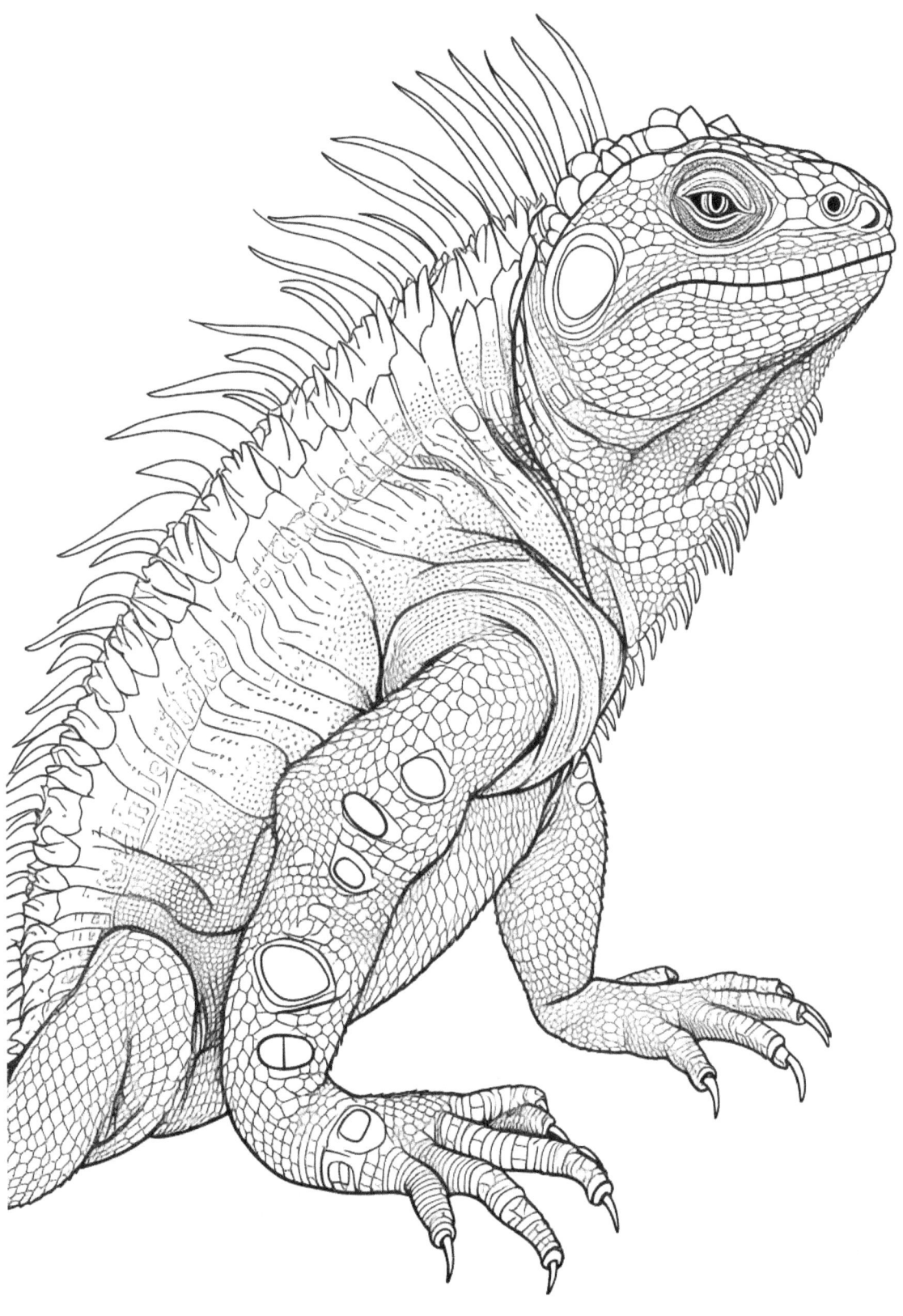

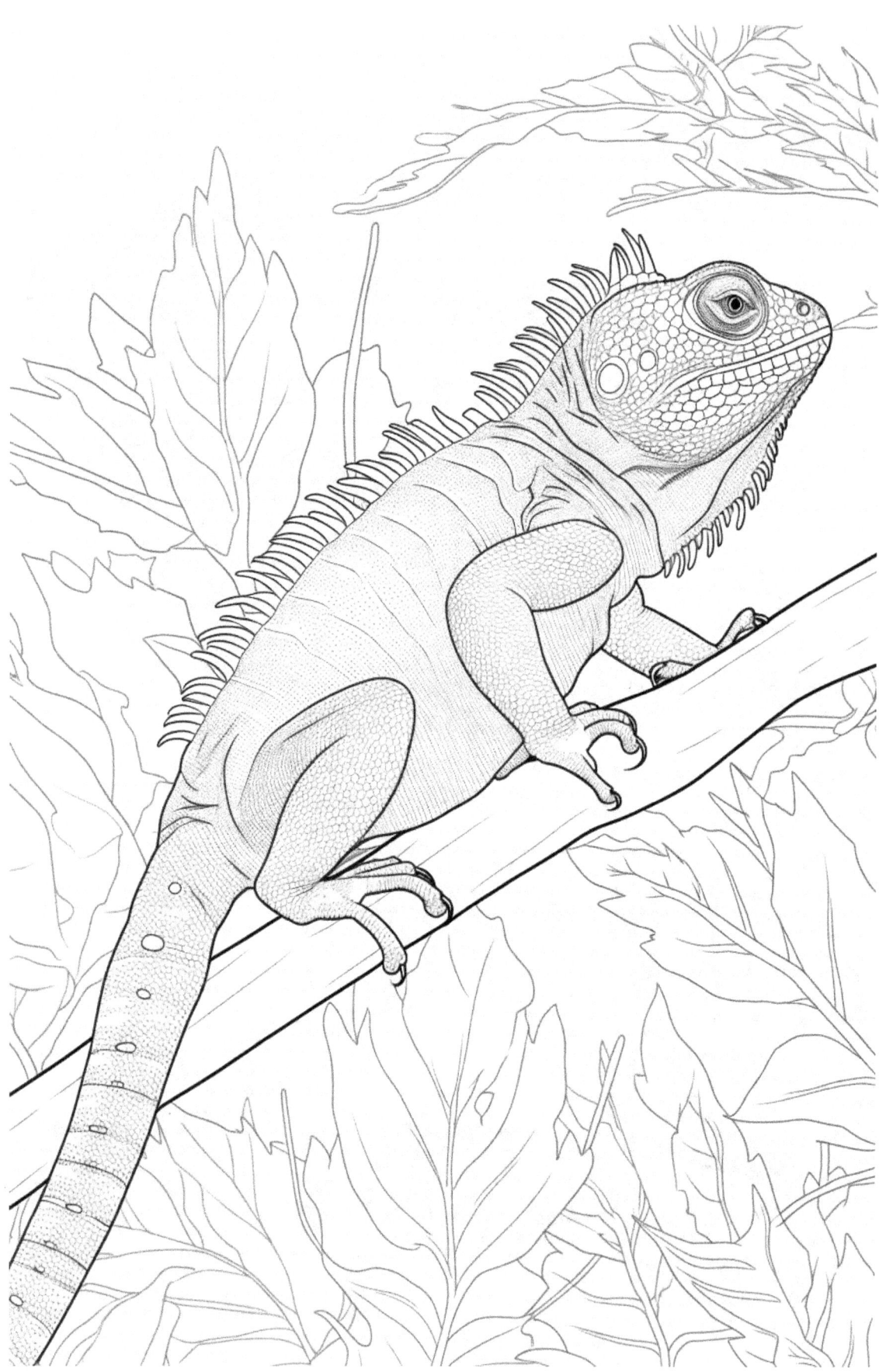

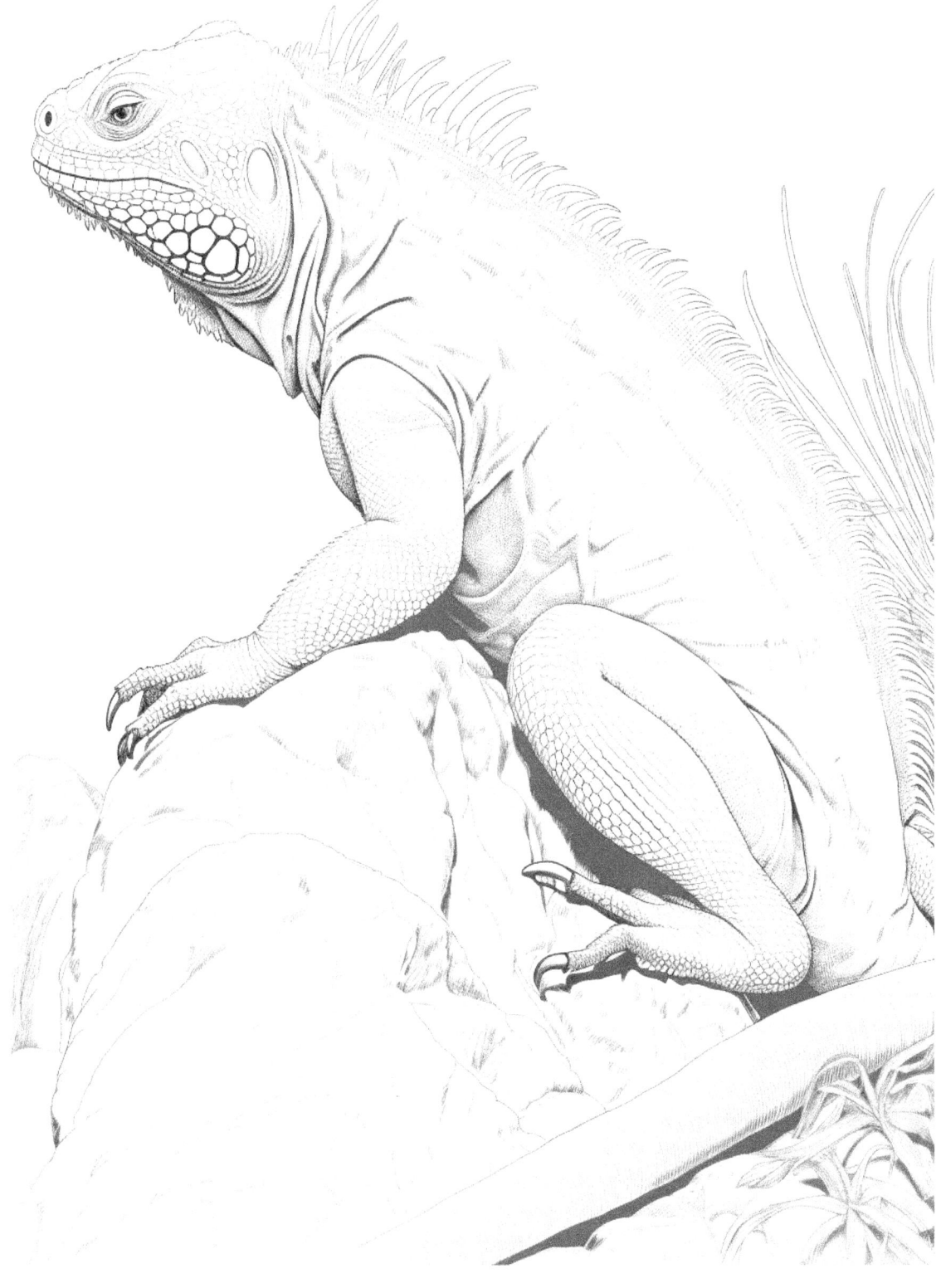

J is for Jaguar

In the lush rainforests of South America, the jaguar proudly roams,

With a coat of spots and muscles strong, they're kings and queens of their homes.

Their sharp senses and stealthy moves help them hunt with ease,

From monkeys swinging in the trees to deer grazing on the leaves.

Jaguars are top predators, but they also play a vital role,

In maintaining the ecosystem and keeping it whole.

With few natural predators their populations do thrive,

A jaguar is a marvelous creature, one that makes us feel alive.

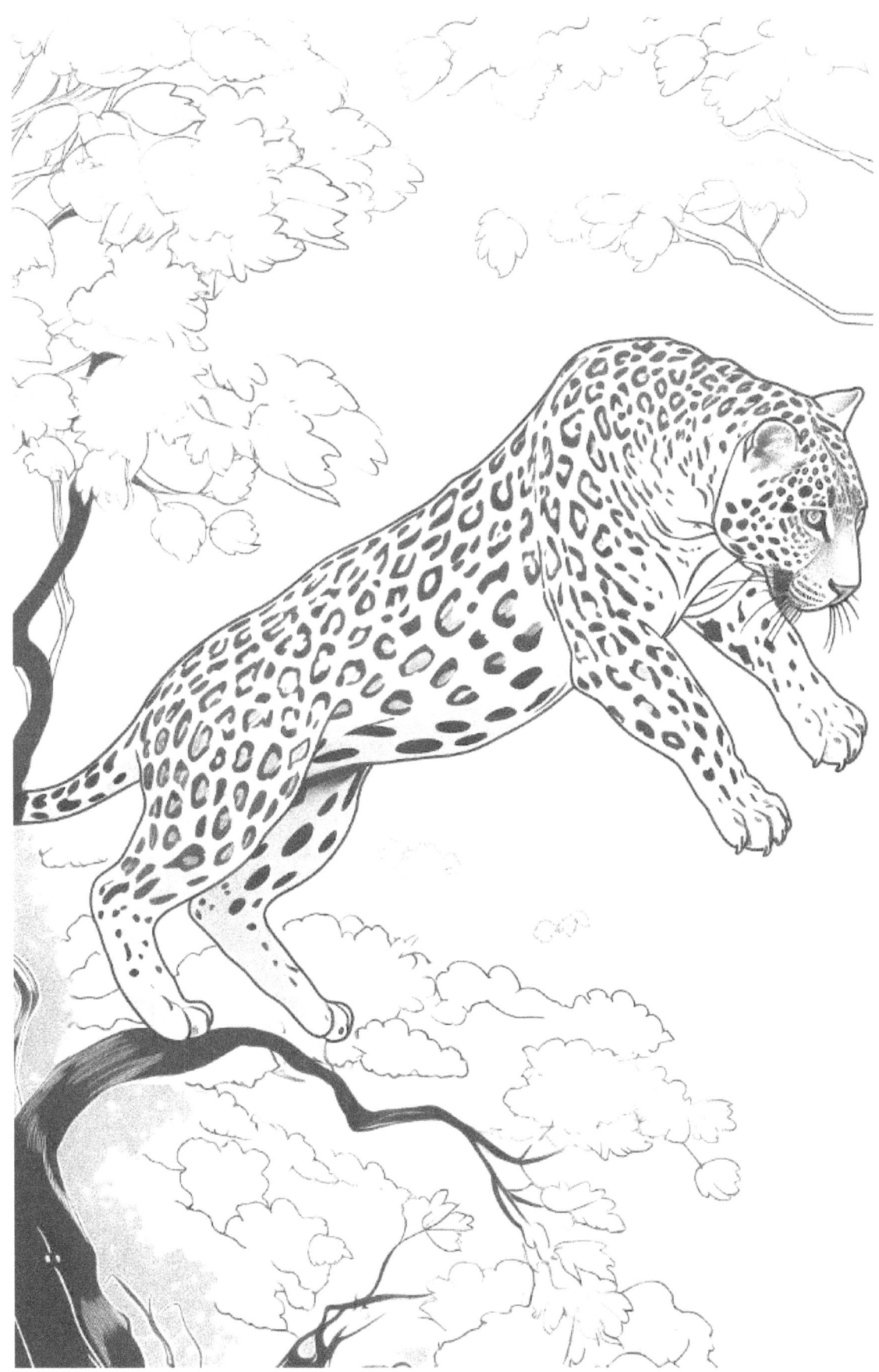

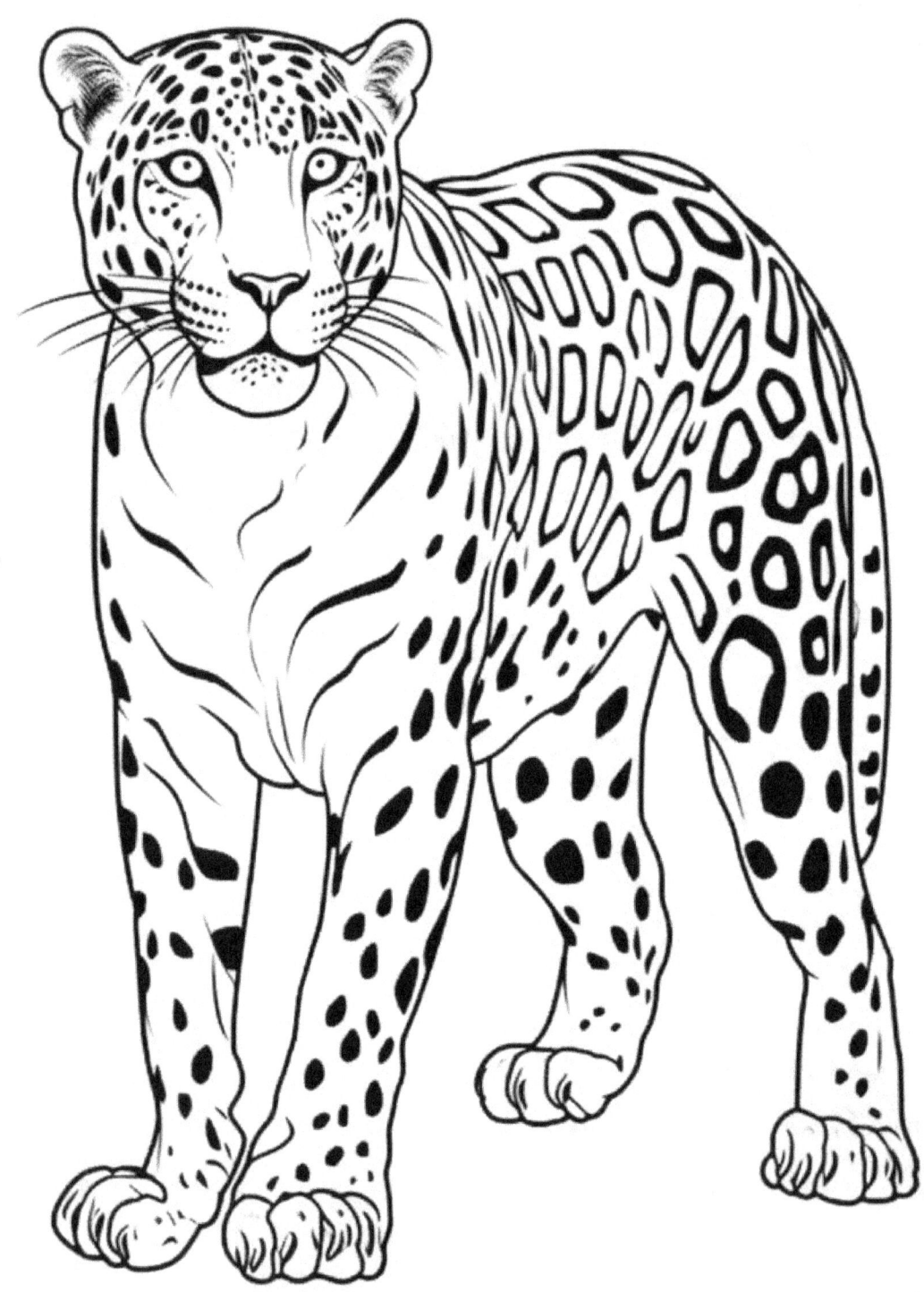

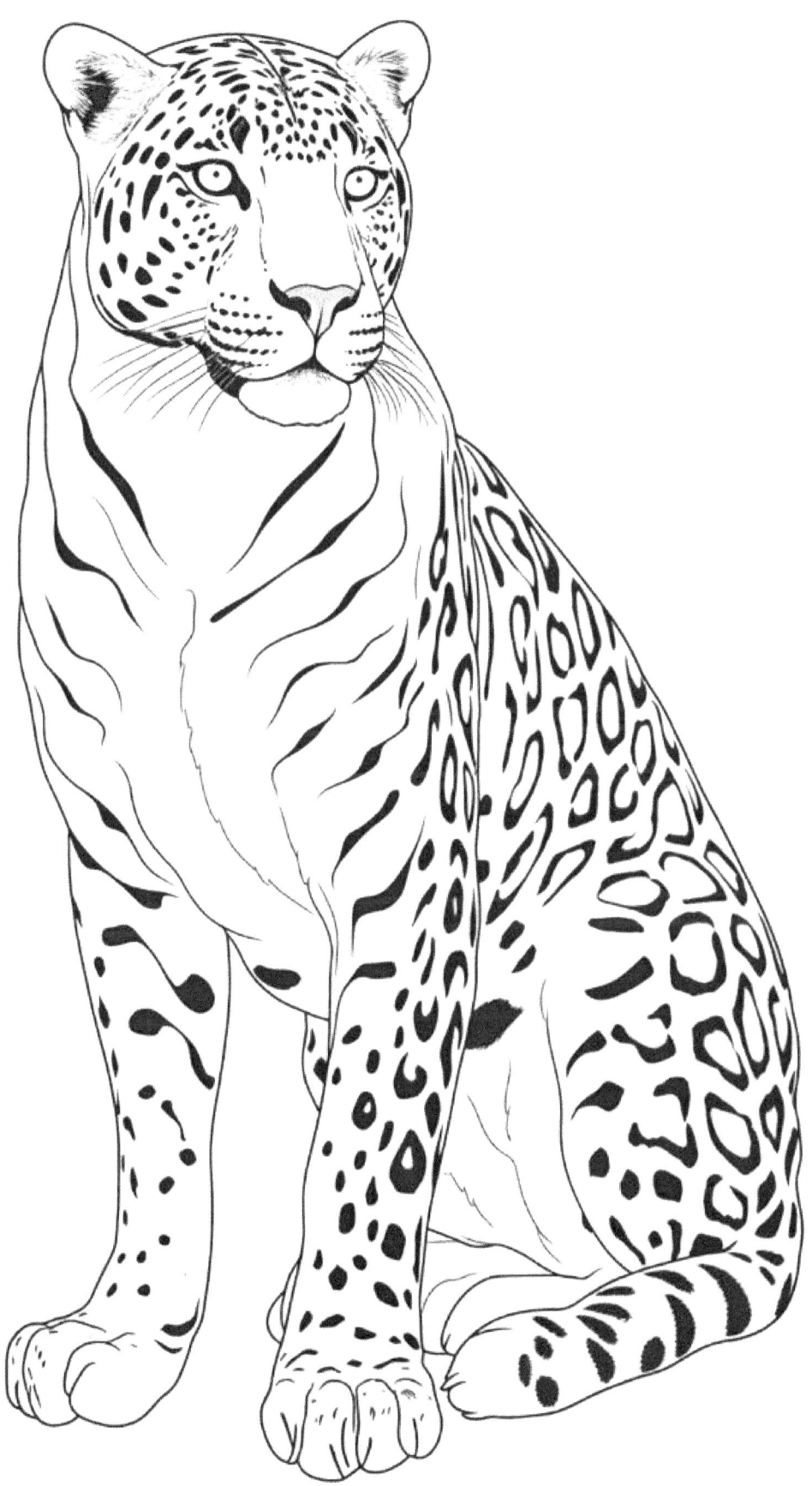

K is for Koi

In the ponds and lakes of Asia, the koi swim and they glide,

With their vibrant colors and patterns, they're creatures of beauty and pride.

They're omnivores that eat plants and insects, and even small fish too,

And with their long lifespan, decades can be lived right through.

Koi are social creatures, often kept in groups in large ponds,

And with their calm nature and grace, they're fish that form bonds.

Most communities of Koi are actively protected,

A koi is a stunning creature, one that's beauty is respected.

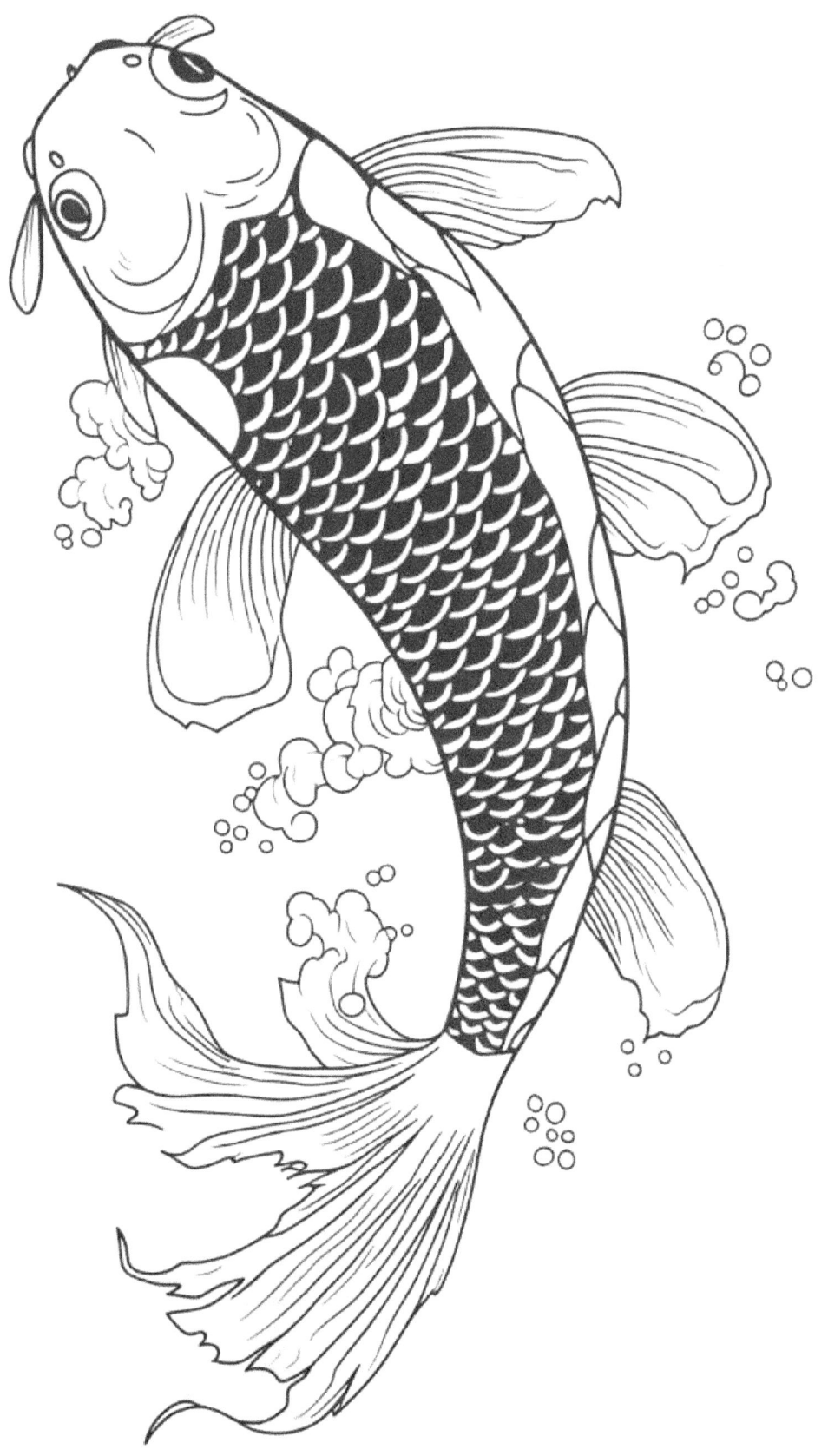

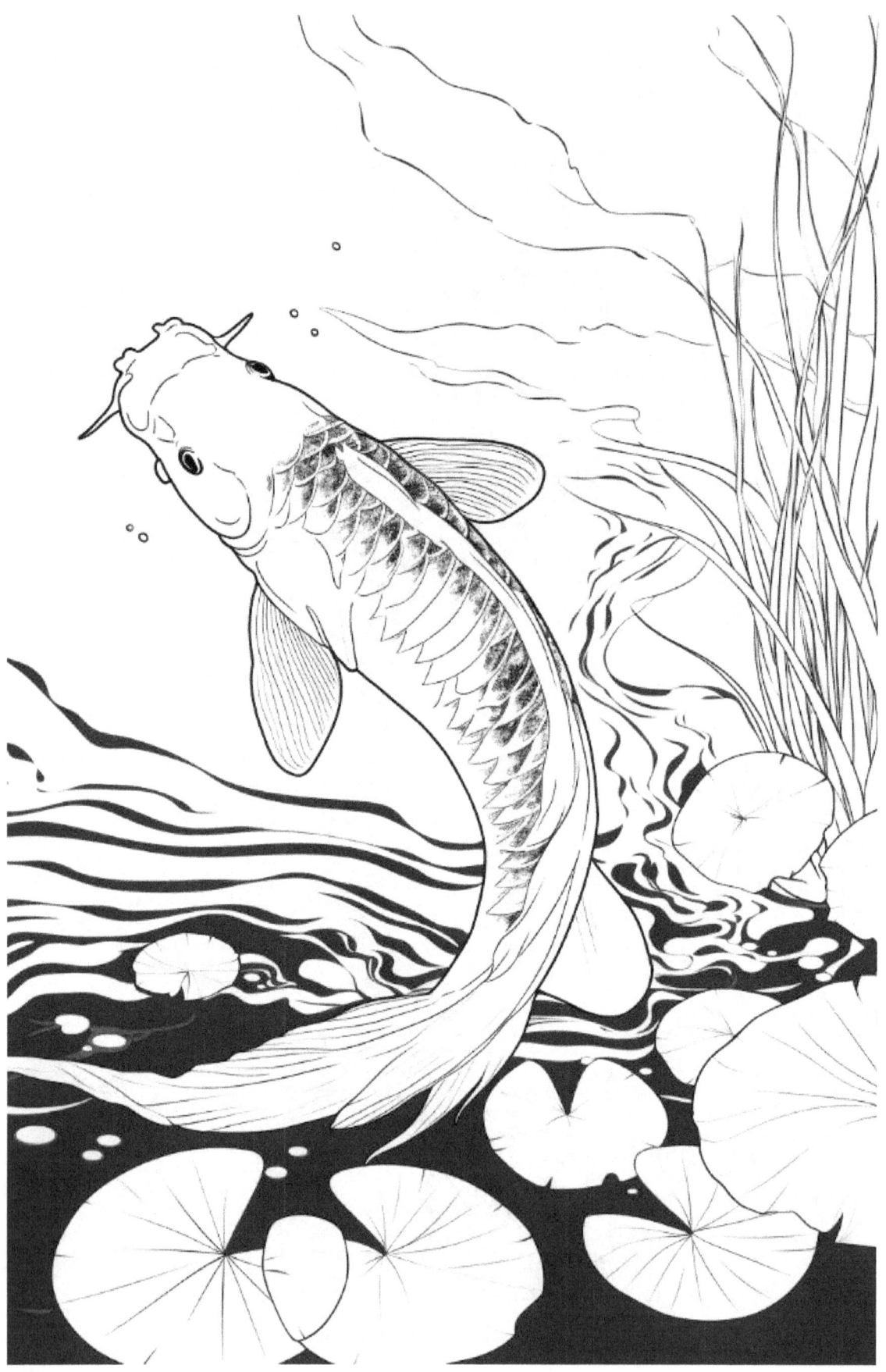

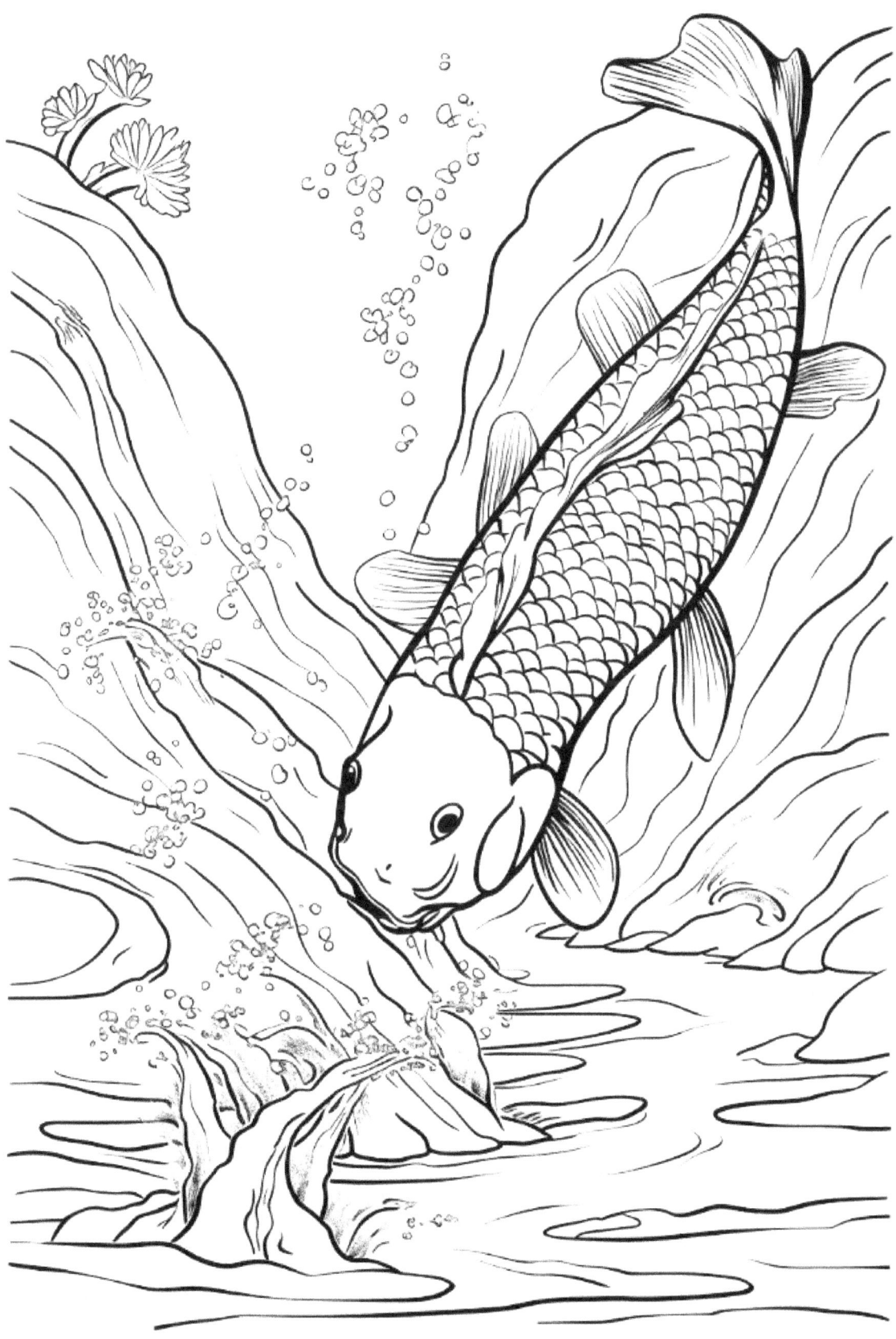

L is for Lion

The lion is a mighty cat, with a mane that's sure to impress,

Roaming the savannah with pride, they're a true king of the wilderness.

They hunt in groups called prides, with the females doing the work,

While the males stand guard and roar, trying to look like a big, tough jerk.

Lions communicate with each other, with a range of growls and roars,

And when they're feeling playful, they might even roll around on all fours.

So if you ever spot a lion, keep your distance and stay aware,

But don't be afraid to appreciate their majesty, with a little bit of care.

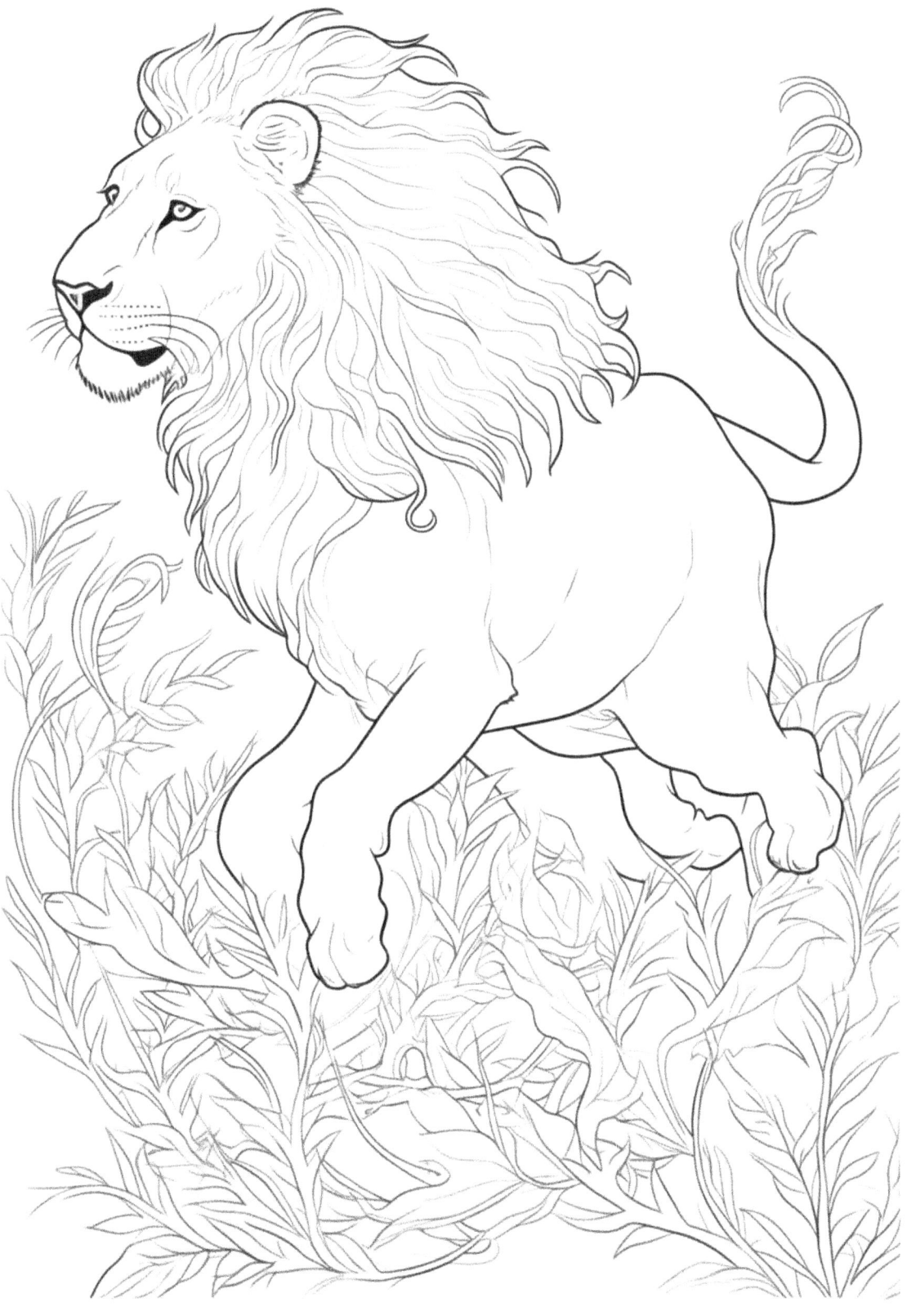

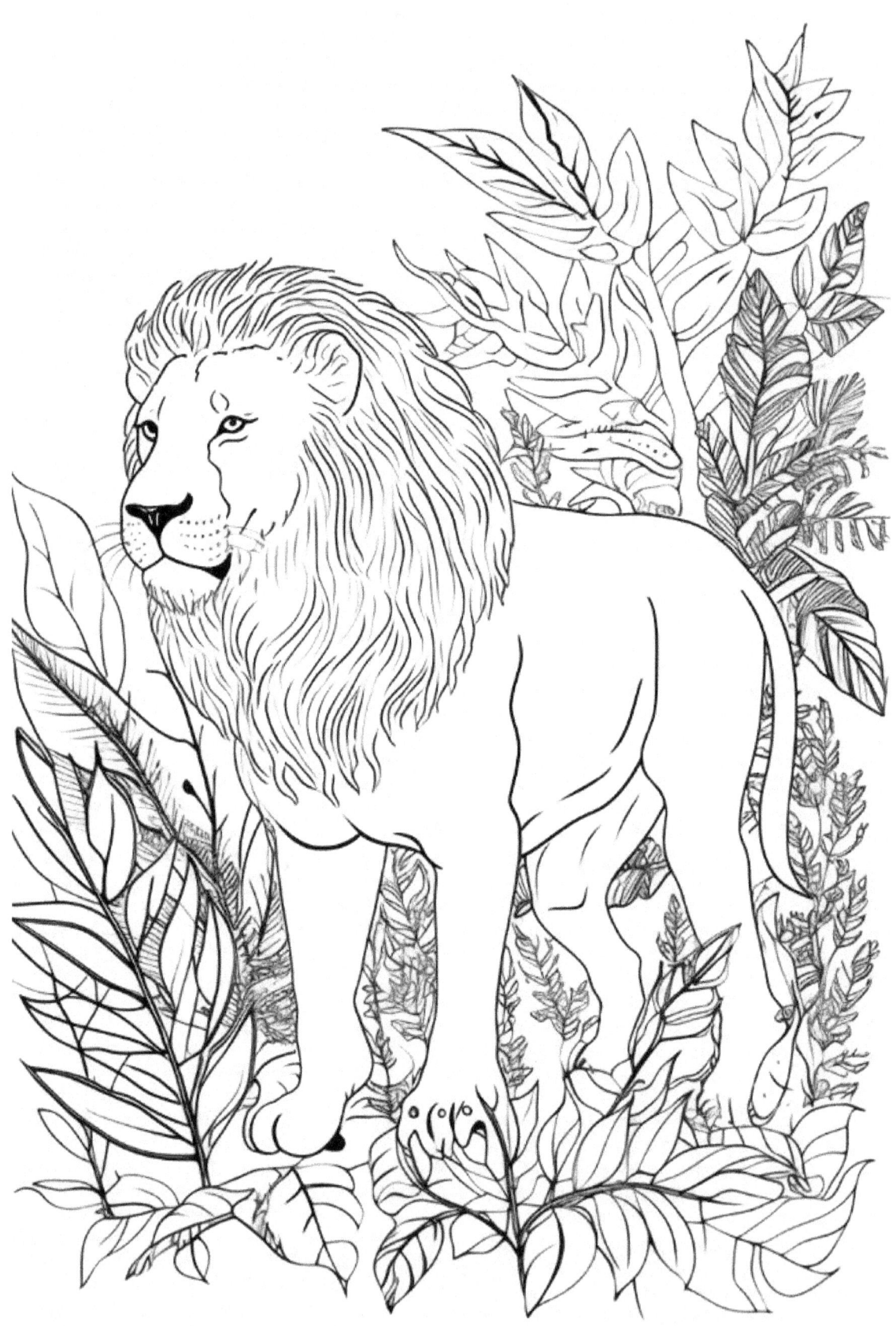

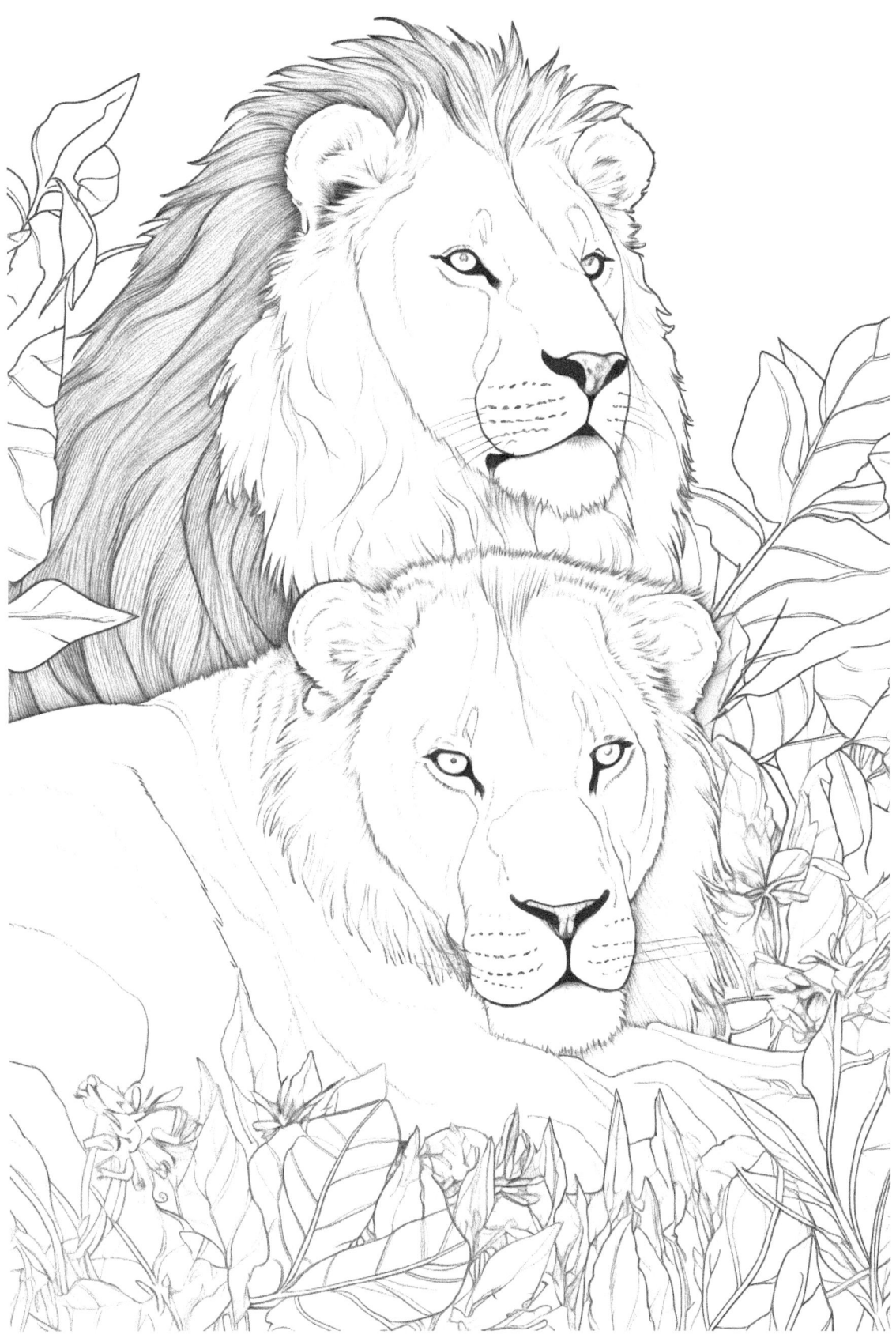

M is for Macaw

with feathers so bright, from reds to blues, yellows, and greens,

Macaws are the most vibrant birds you've seen!

And when they're happy, they squawk and shout,

Their happiness and energy are contagious, no doubt!

Macaws are social animals and they love to play,

They can mimic sounds and words that we say.

They fly in flocks and mate for life,

 Their bond is strong, no need for strife!

Let's protect these birds, their homes, and their space,

And let the Macaws fly free with grace!

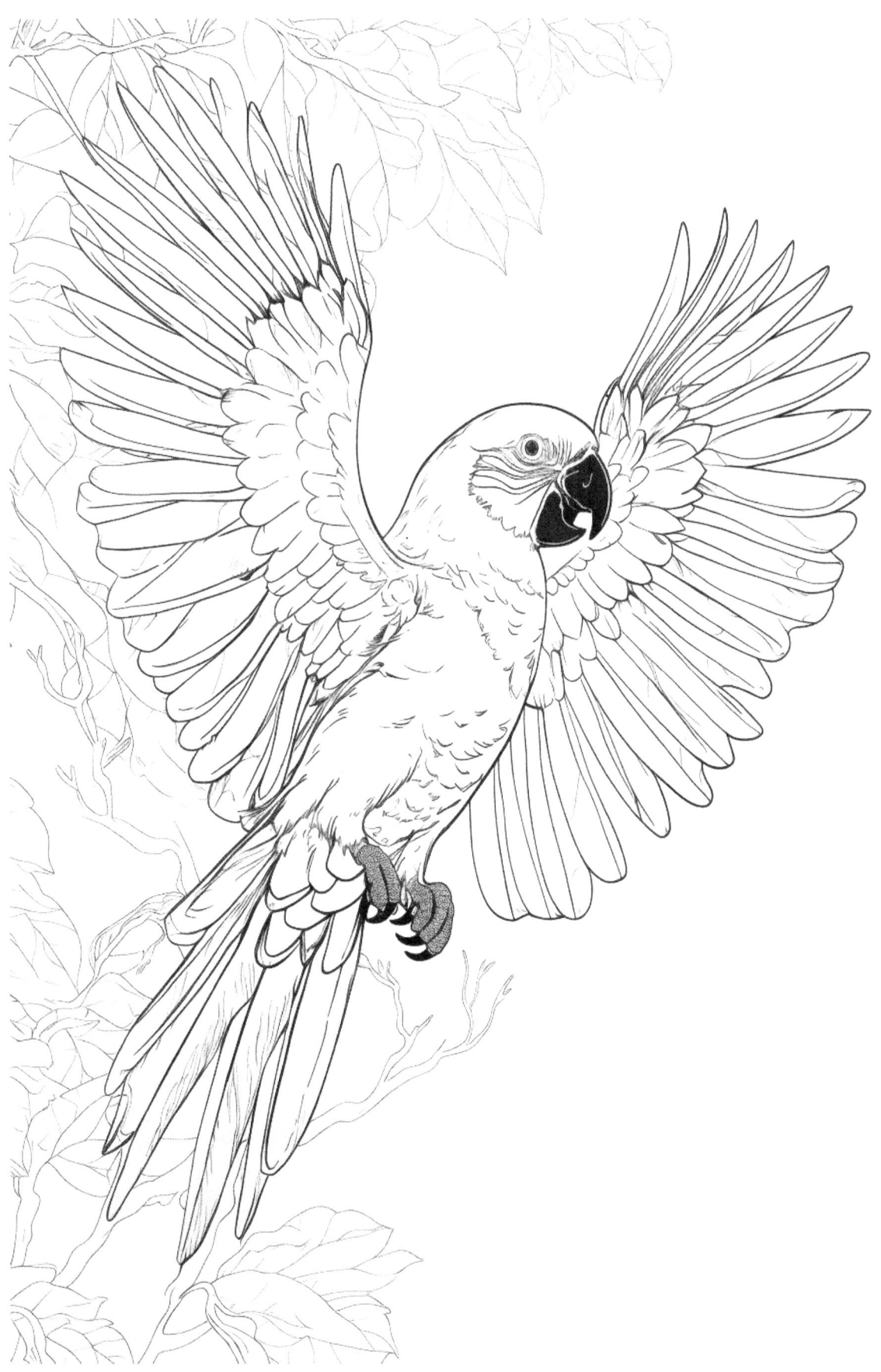

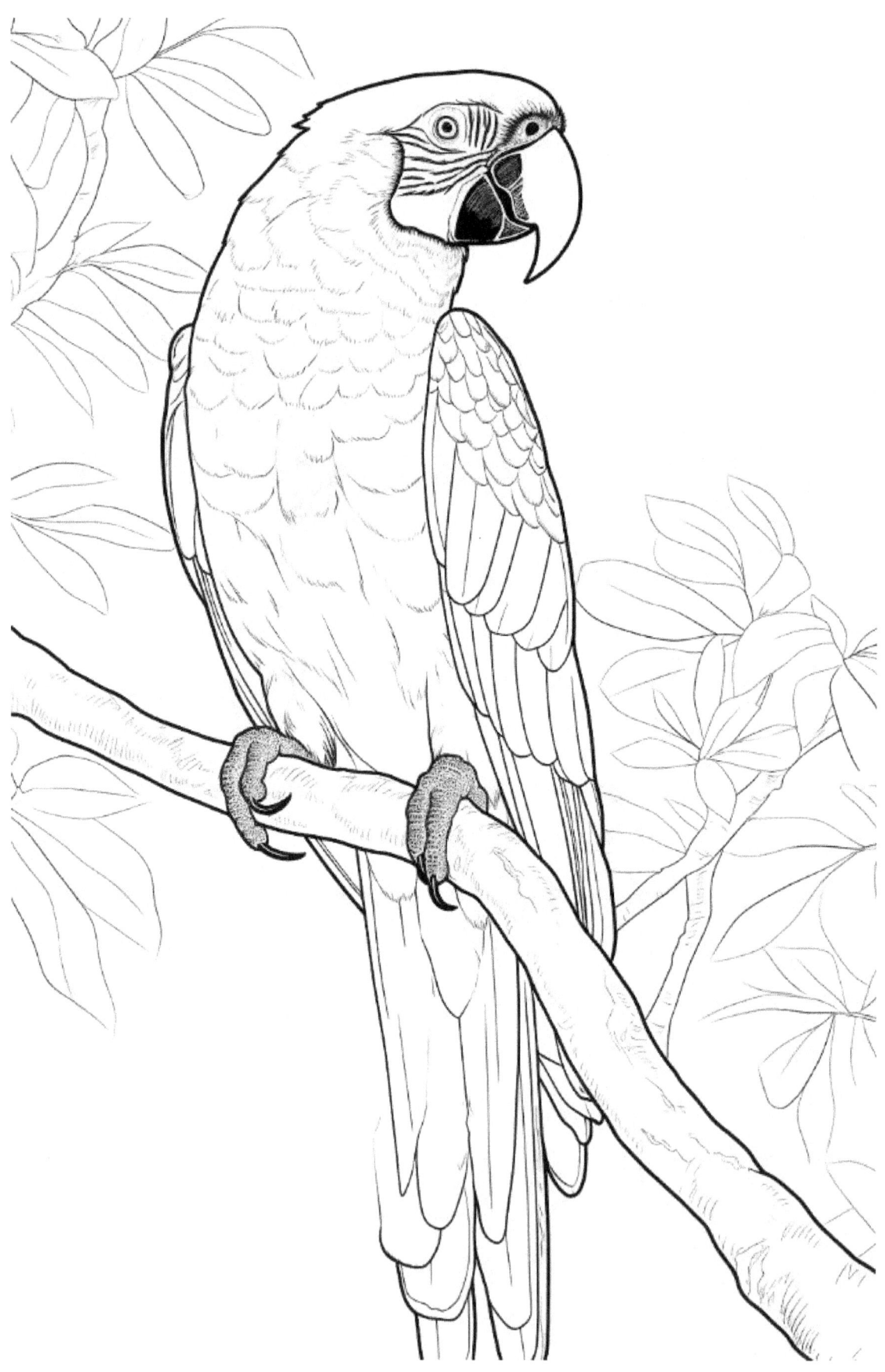

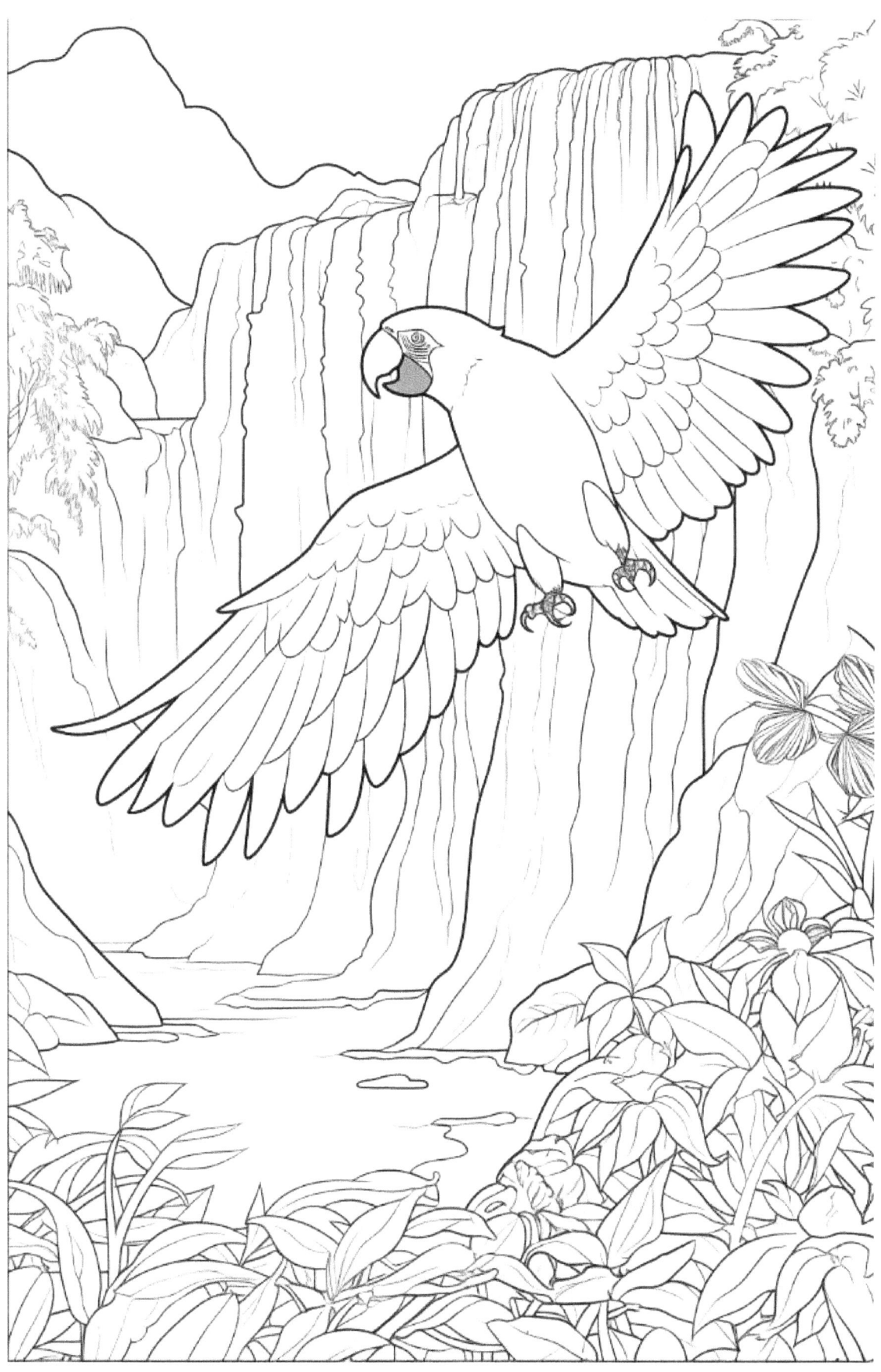

N is for Nightingale

A bird with a sweet natural melody,

In the woods and gardens of Europe, its supplies harmony.

They have brown and gray feathers, with a hooked beak for prey,

And with their soothing voice and range, they sing night and day.

Nightingales feed on insects, worms, and even some fruits,

And with their unique sound and talent, they're birds of repute.

These birds are also known for their long seasonal migration,

Traveling thousands of miles, without a moment's hesitation.

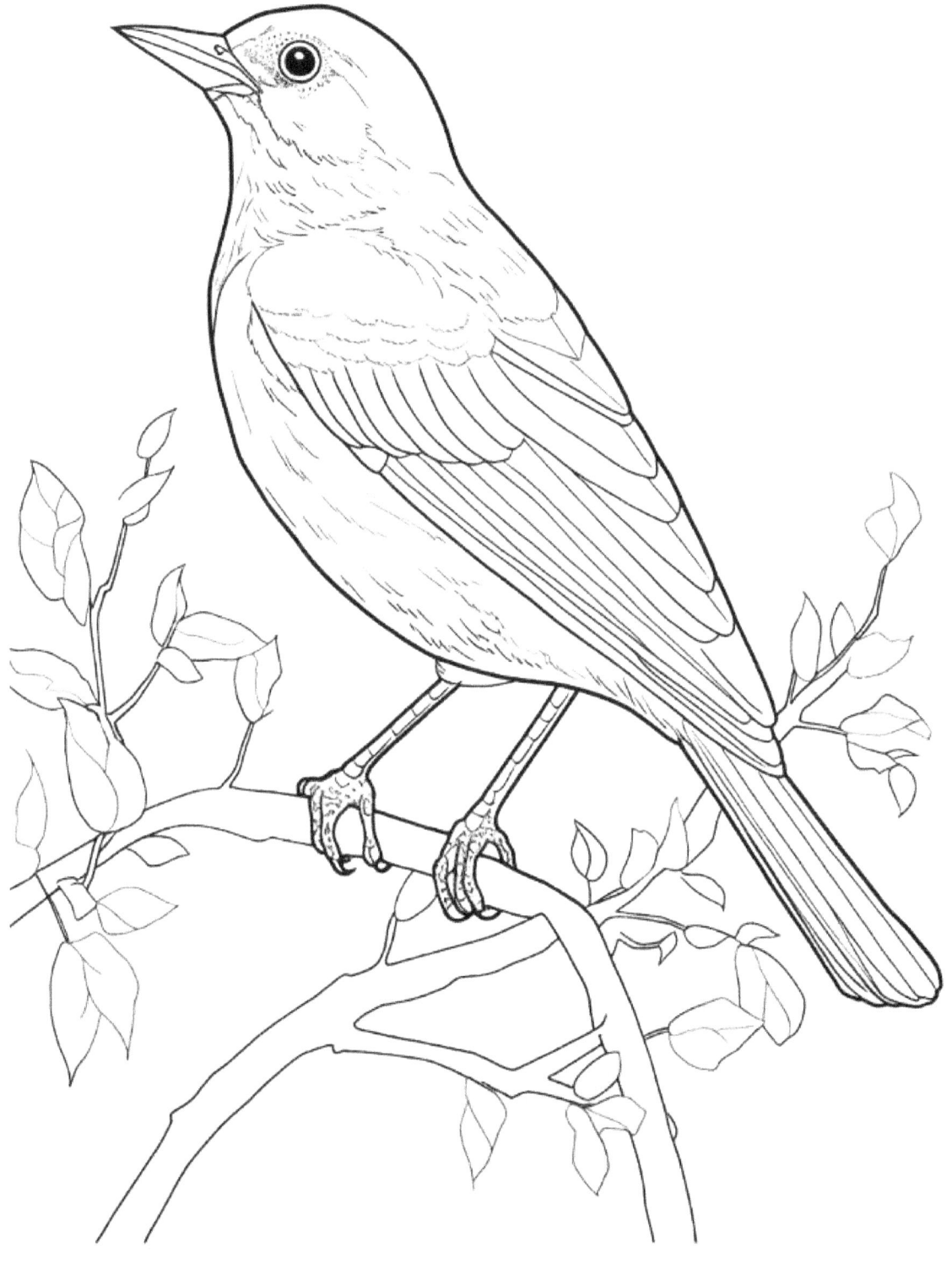

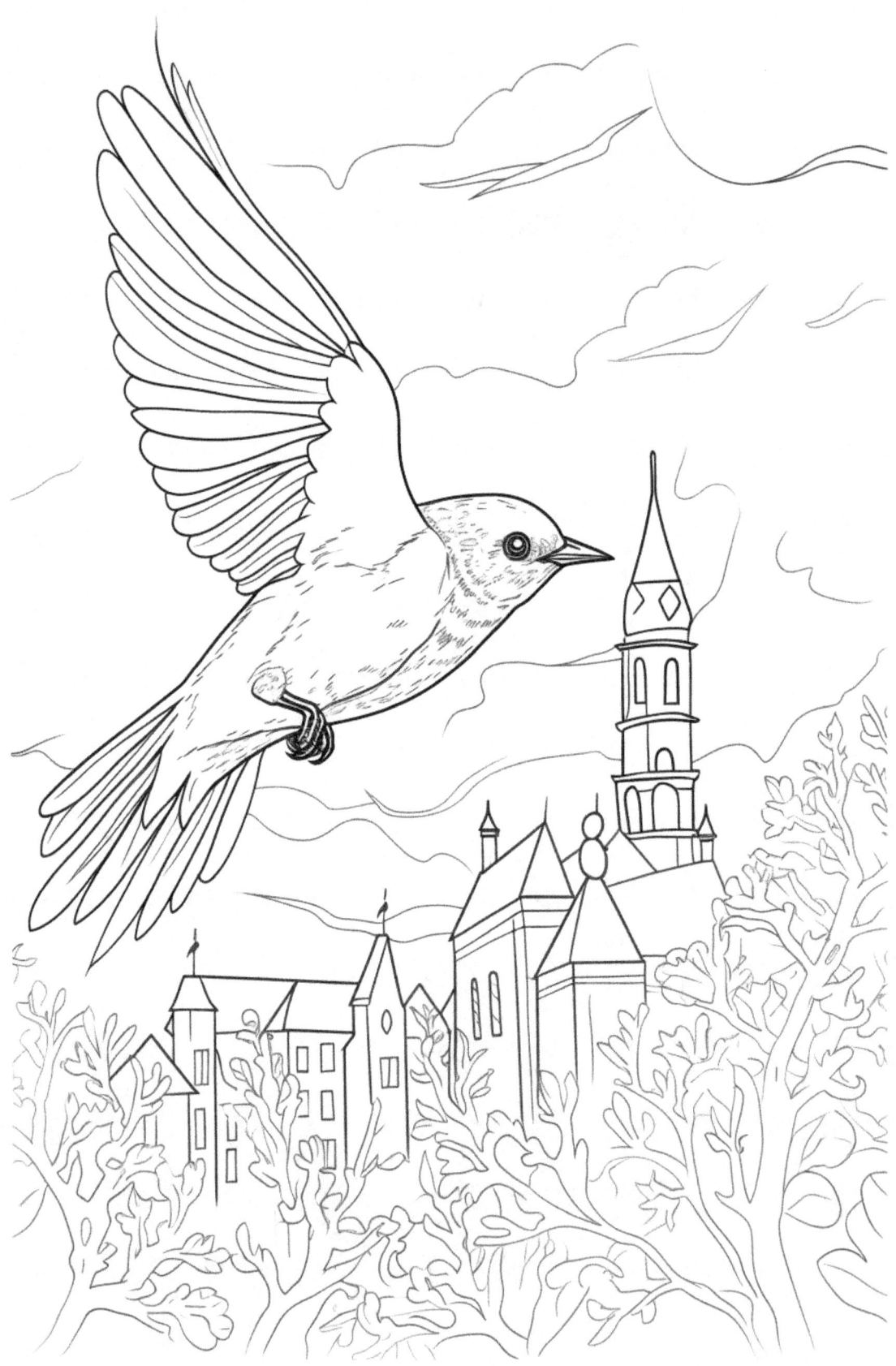

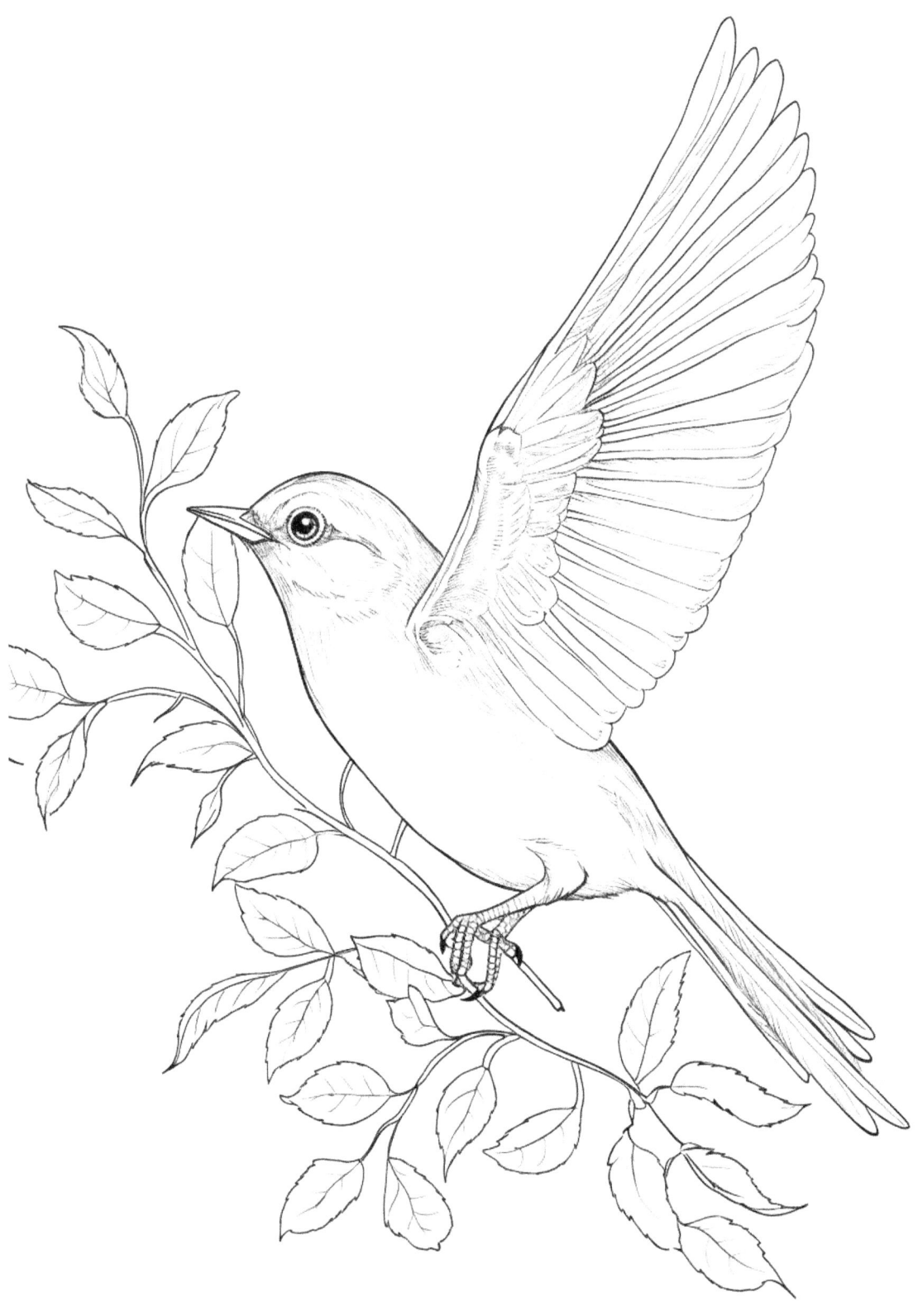

O is for Ocelot

a feline that's as sleek as it's shy,

Found in Central and South America, where it hides when it spies.

From rodents to reptiles, they eat a varied diet,

And with their sharp teeth and strong jaws, it's easy to bite it.

Ocelots are solitary, roaming at night with grace,

And with their spotted coats and long tails, they're a sight to embrace.

They eat small mammals and birds, and even fish in tough times,

And with their sharp claws, any tree they can climb.

Their fur is soft and silky, their spots are so neat,

And when they're feeling playful, they pounce with nimble feet!

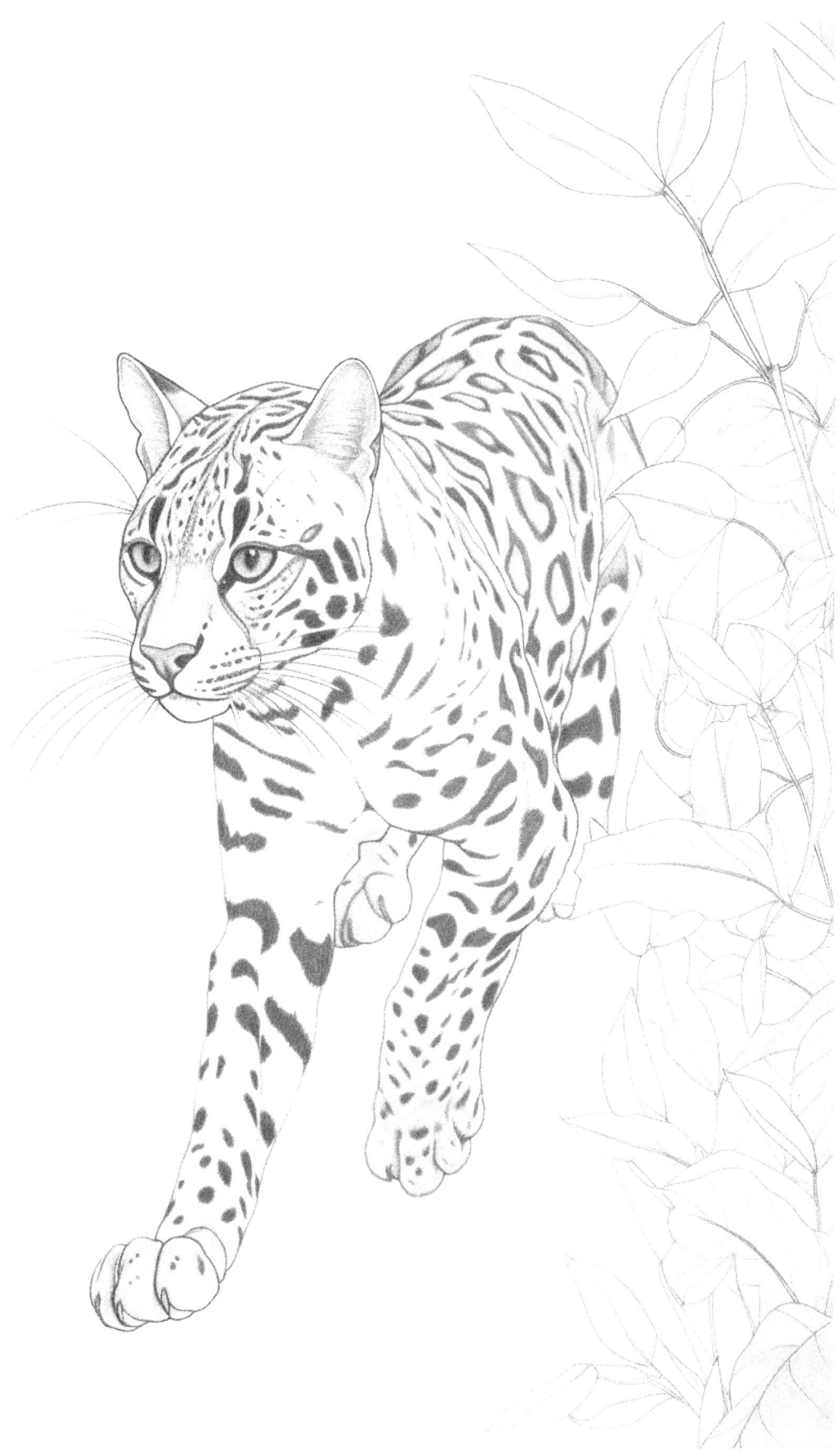

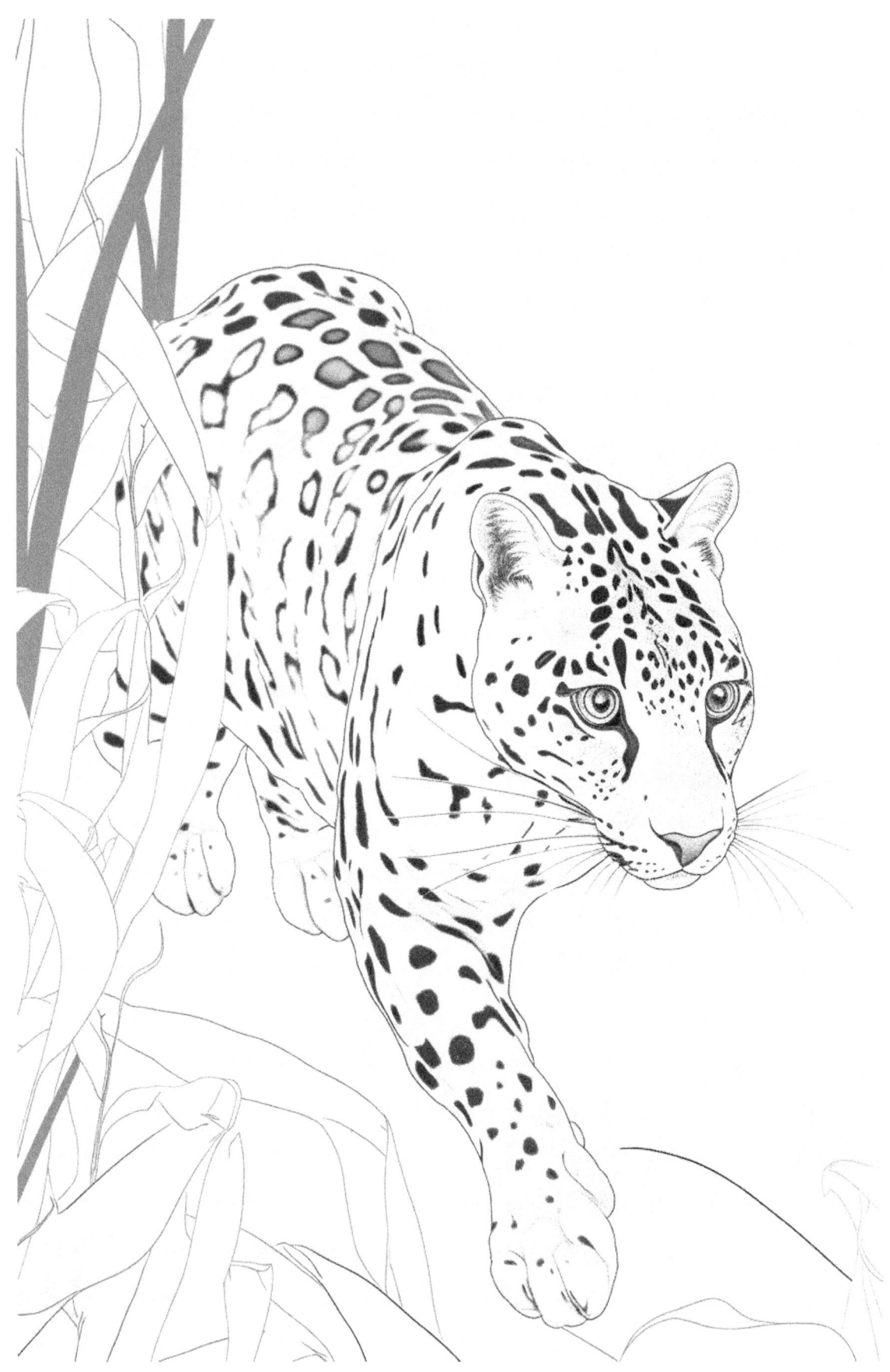

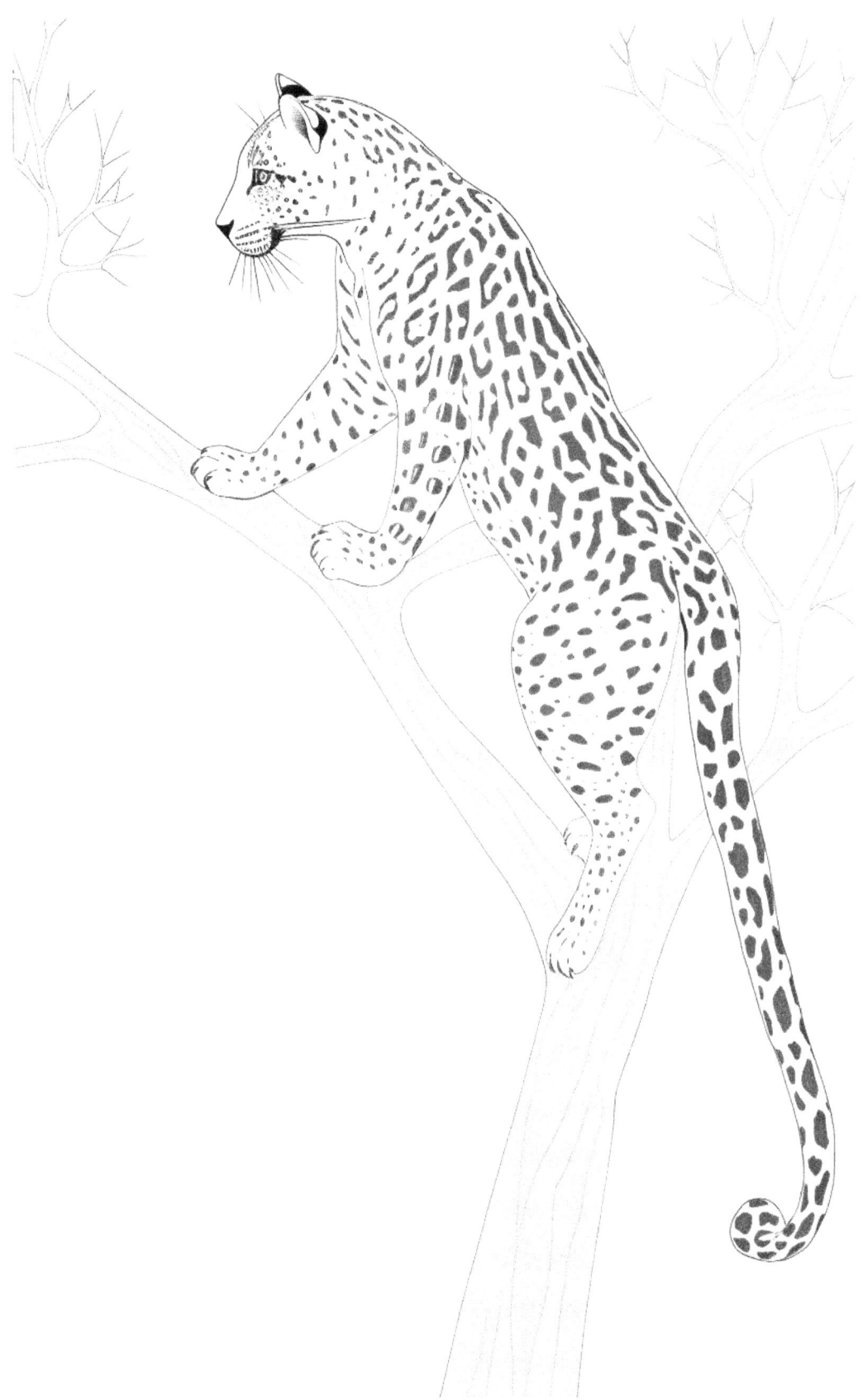

P is for Penguin

In the icy regions of Antarctica, the penguin waddles, and slides,

With their sleek feathers and streamlined shape, they're creatures that glide.

Penguins are skillful hunters, they eat fish, krill and squid,

And they have a special gland to get rid of salt, so that's what they did.

Penguins huddle in groups to stay warm in the cold, snowy weather,

And with their unique adaptations, they're always together.

So if you see a penguin, give them a wave and say hi,

They'll likely waddle over and give you a friendly high-five!

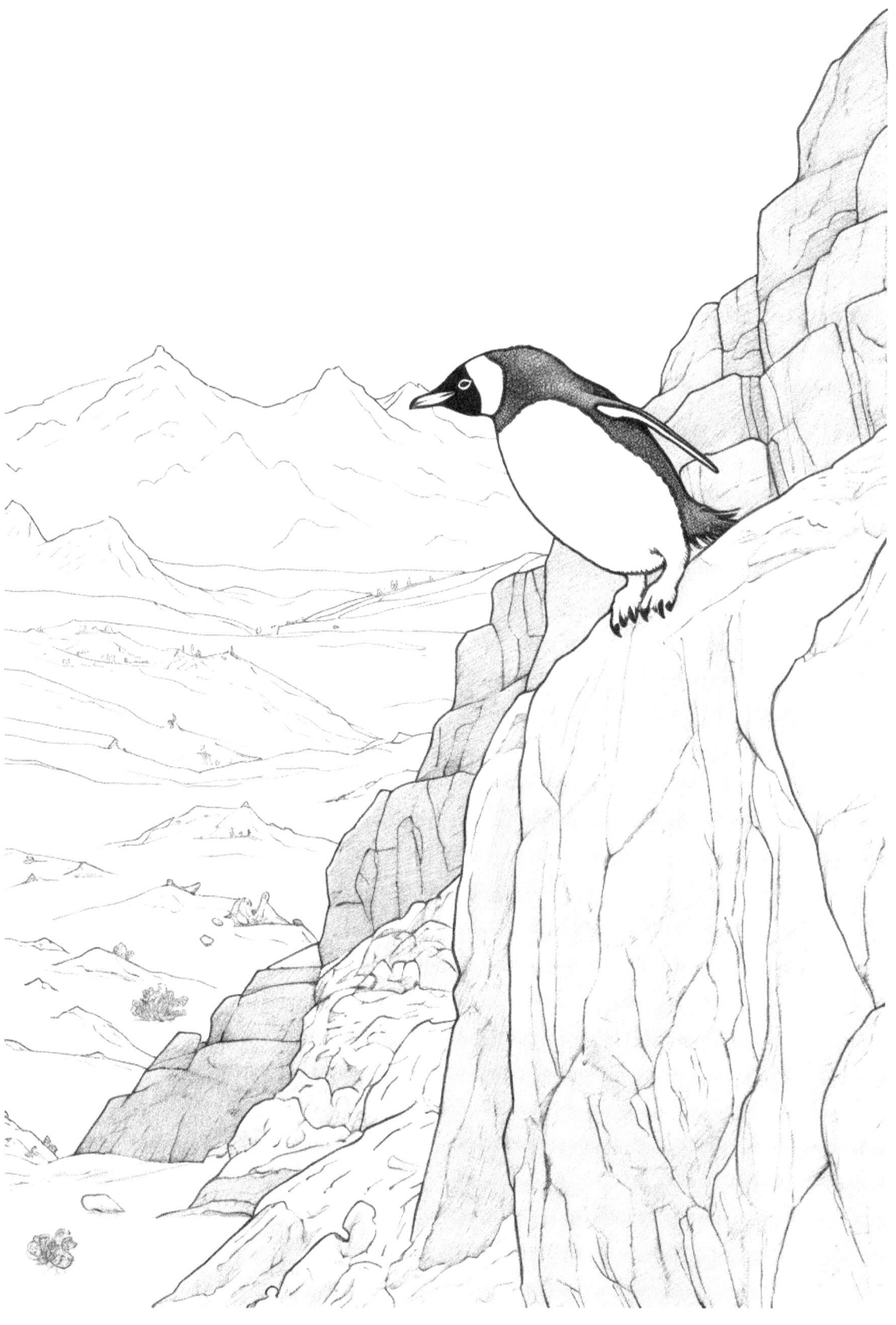

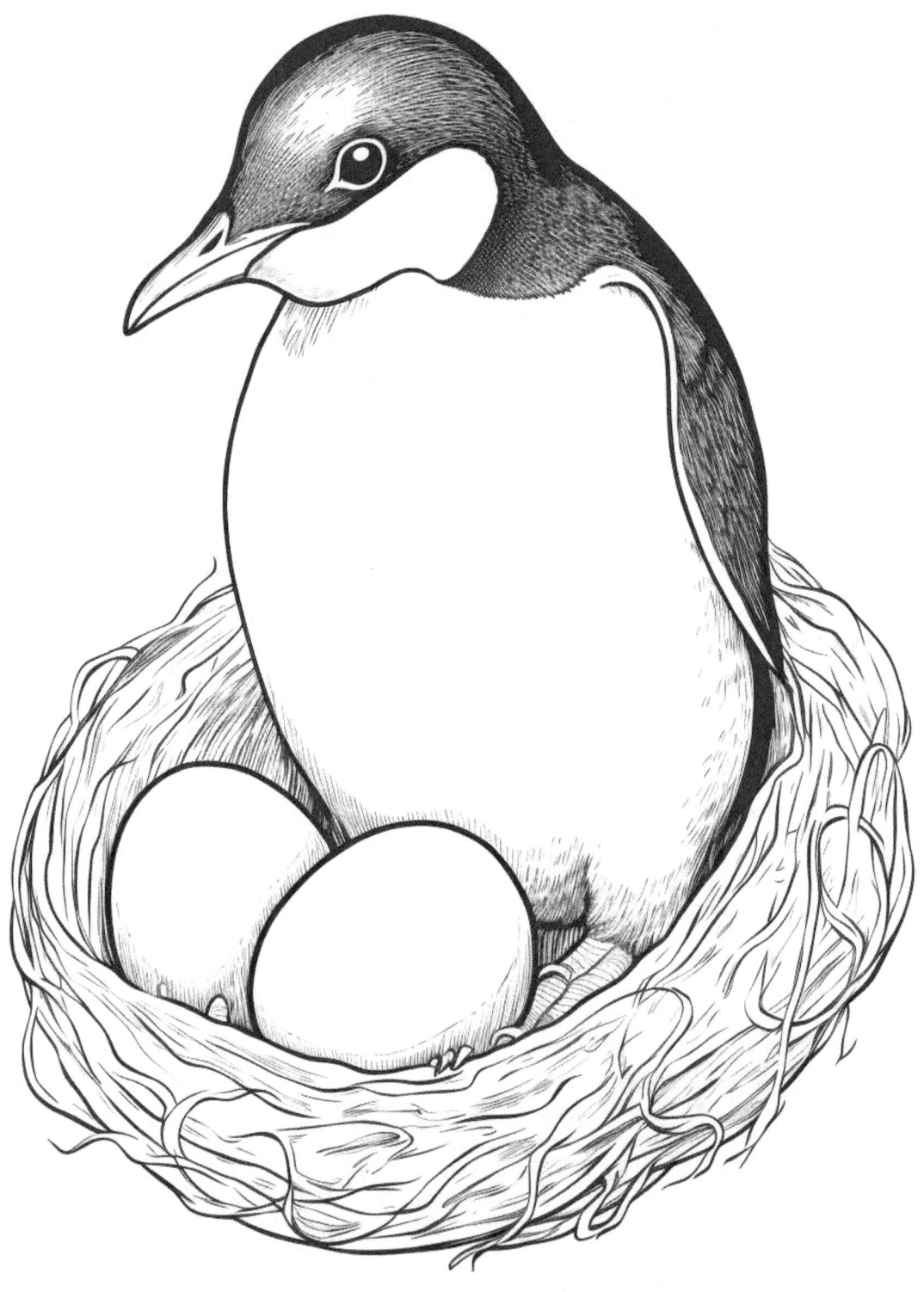

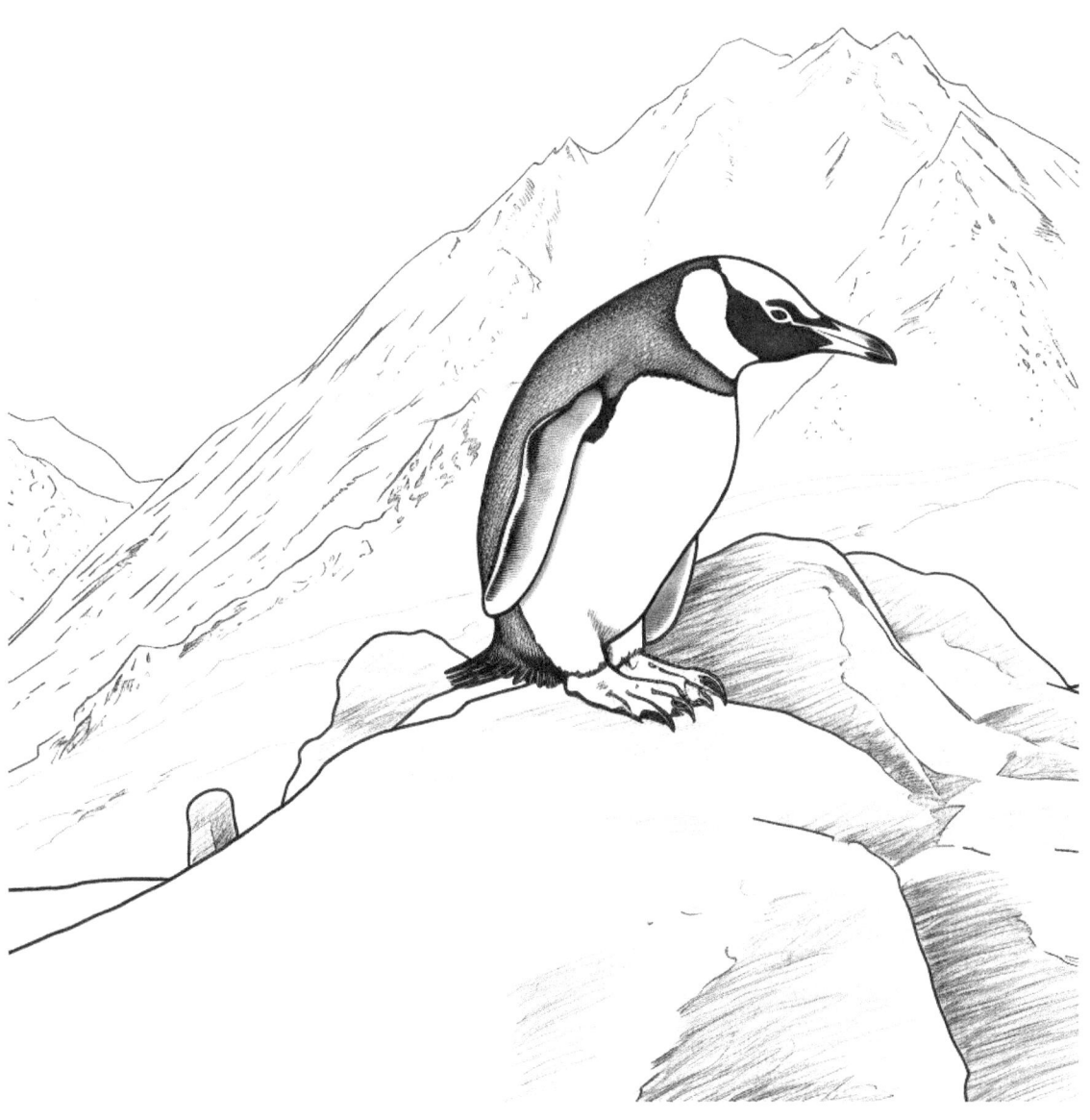

Q is for Quail

In the fields and meadows, the quail scurries, and dashes,

With their plump bodies and speckled feathers, they're creatures that flash.

They're omnivores that eat seeds, insects, and more,

And with their ground-dwelling habits, they're creatures that explore.

Quails often live in coveys, with their distinct calls and whistles,

And with their camouflage and swift running, they're creatures that sizzle.

So, let's admire them from a distance, and give them their space,

For they're a special part of nature, and worth the embrace.

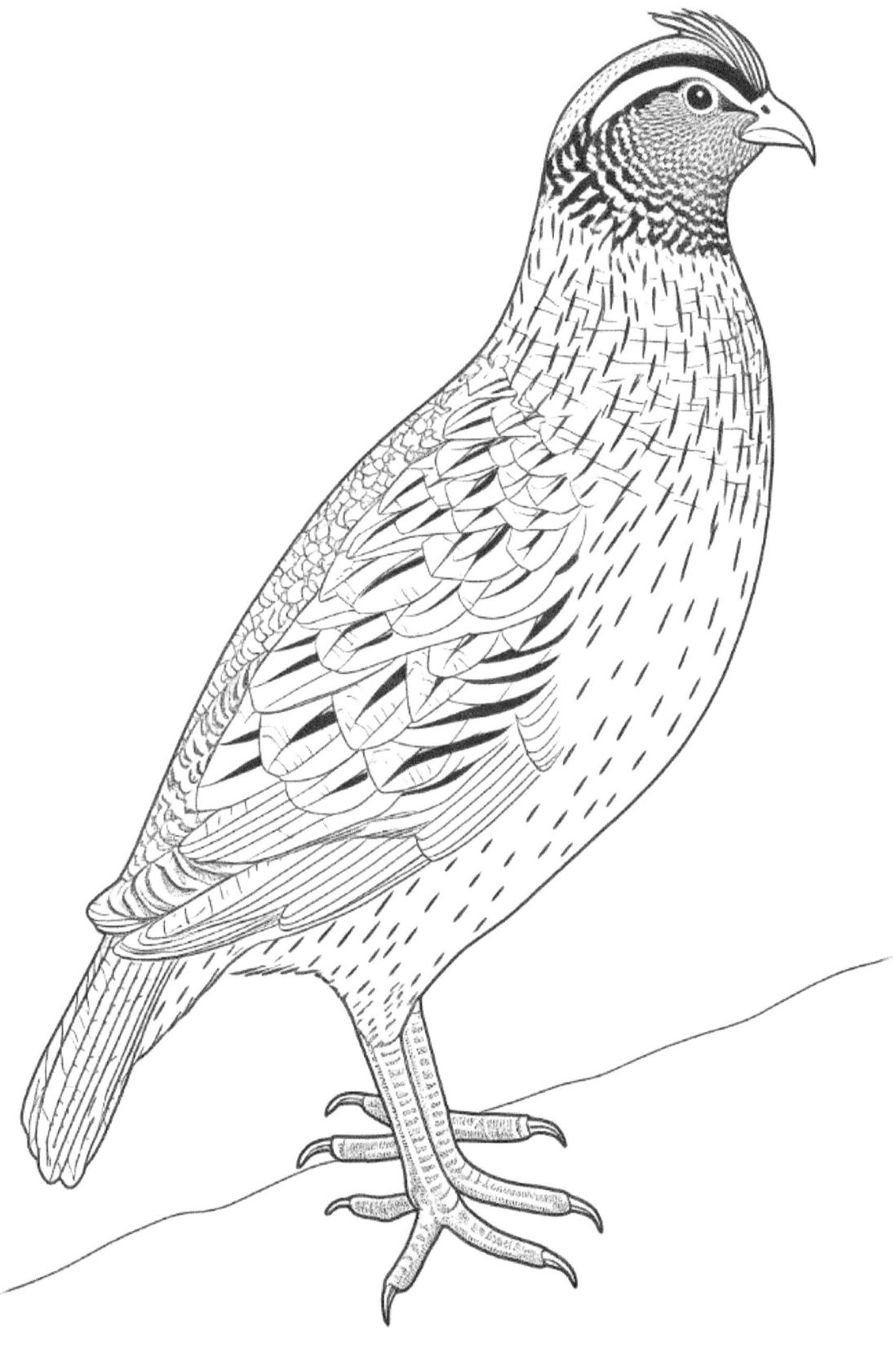

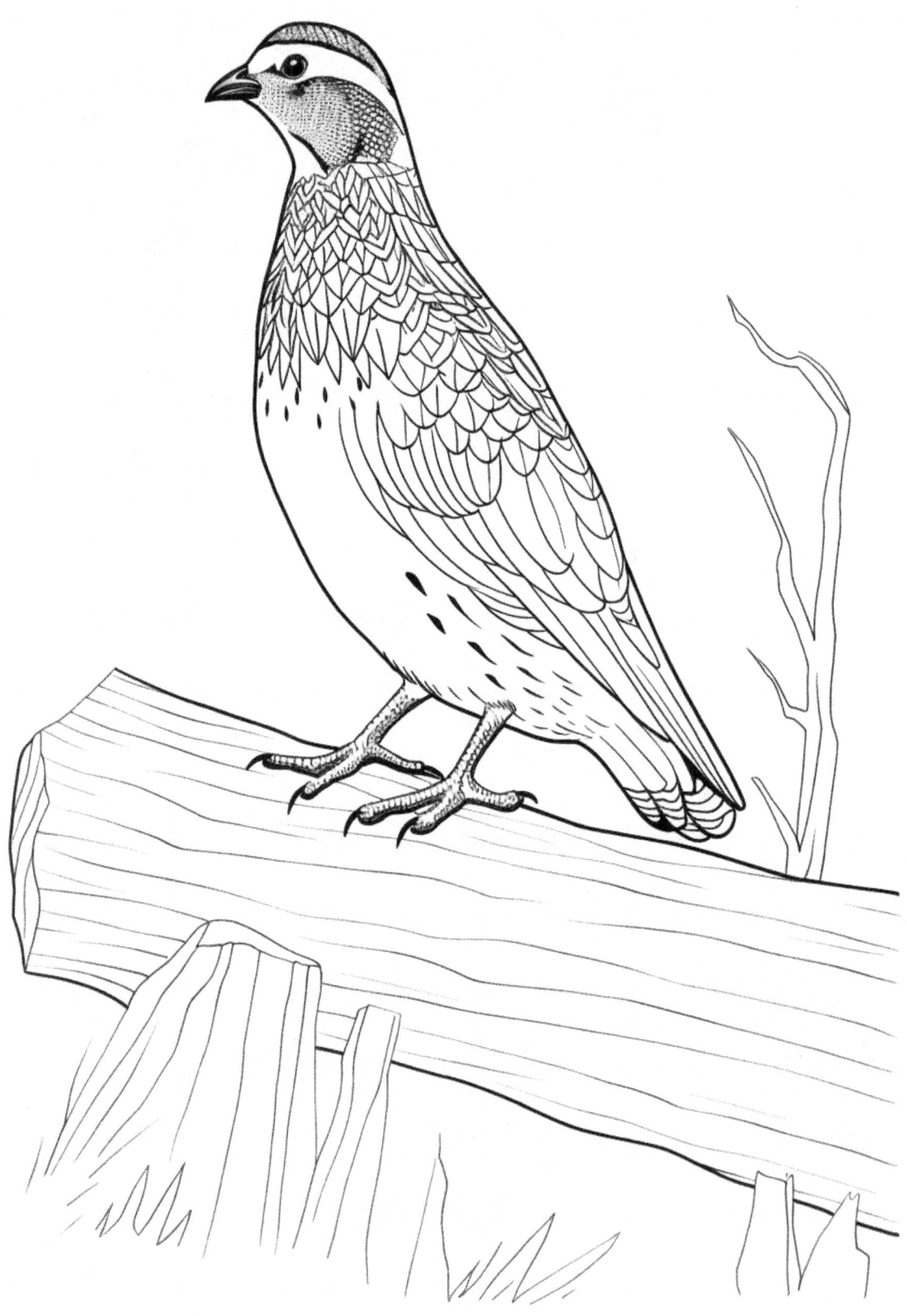

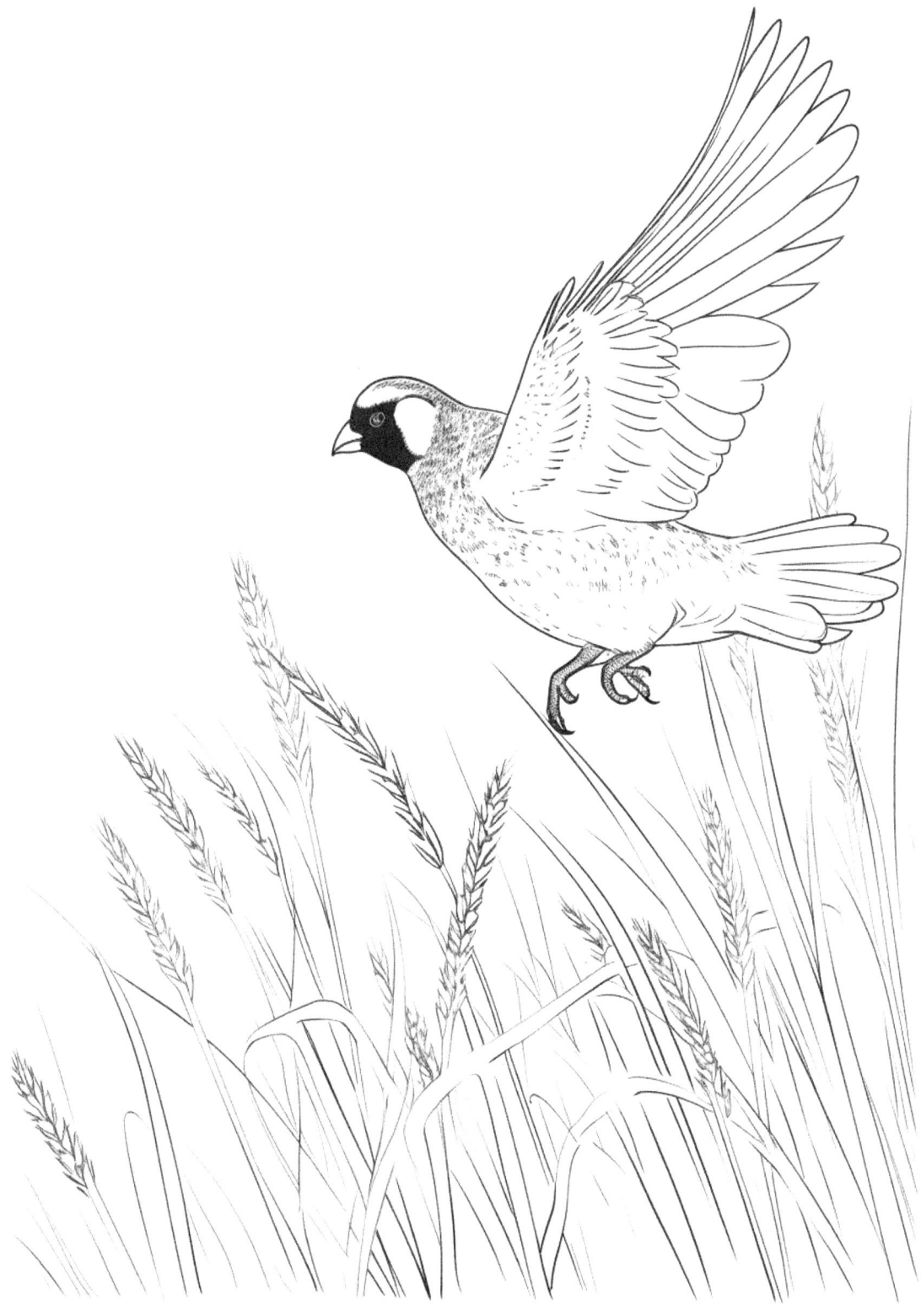

R is for Rhino

In the savanna, the great Rhino roams,

It's a massive beast of an animal with large sturdy bones.

With two horns on their nose, one big and one small,

They're one of the coolest armored land mammals of all!

Their skin is thick, just like a tanks armor plating,

It protects them from predators that may be hiding and waiting.

Rhinos are social creatures that love chase, fight and to play,

They communicate with grunts to their friends and talk all day!

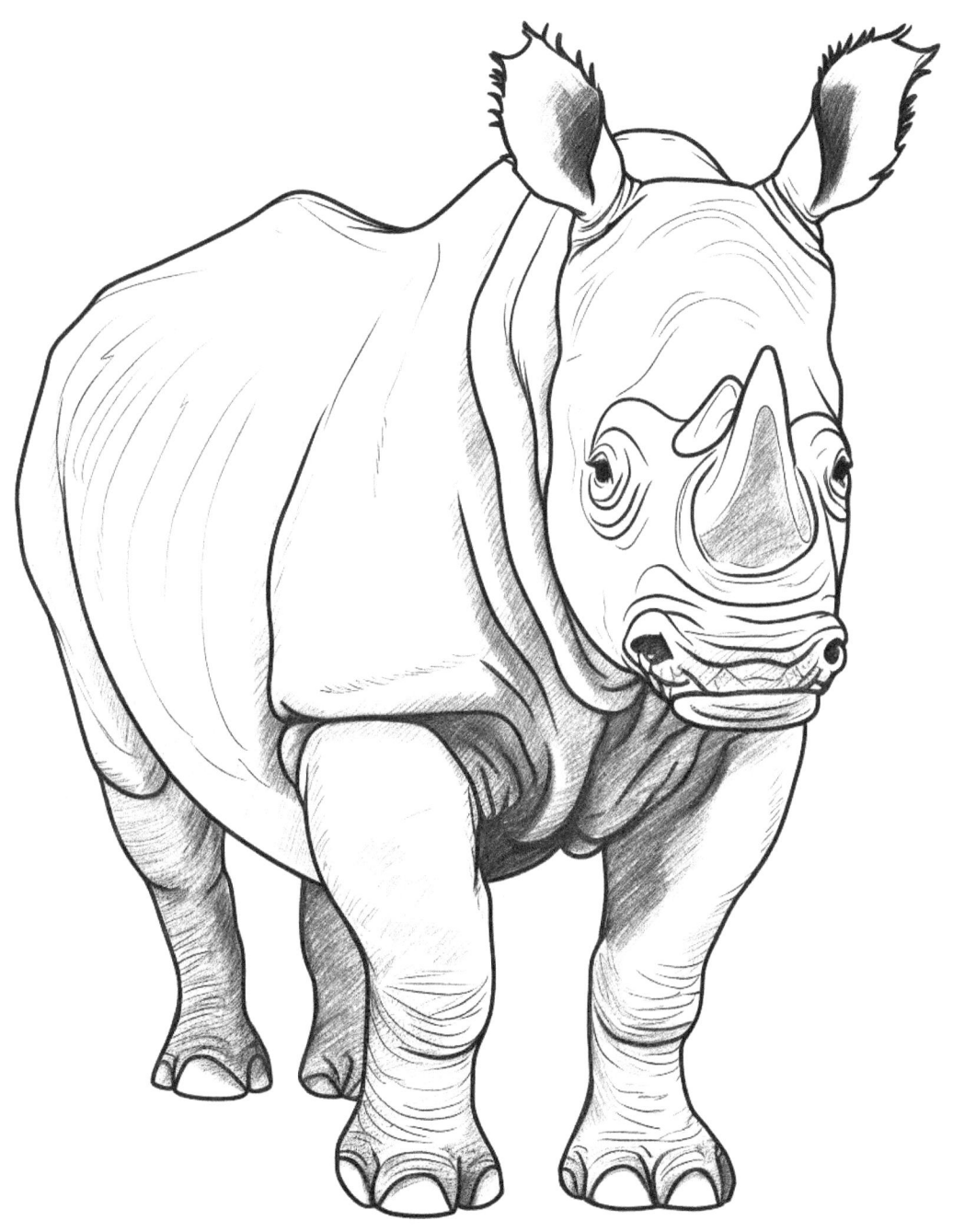

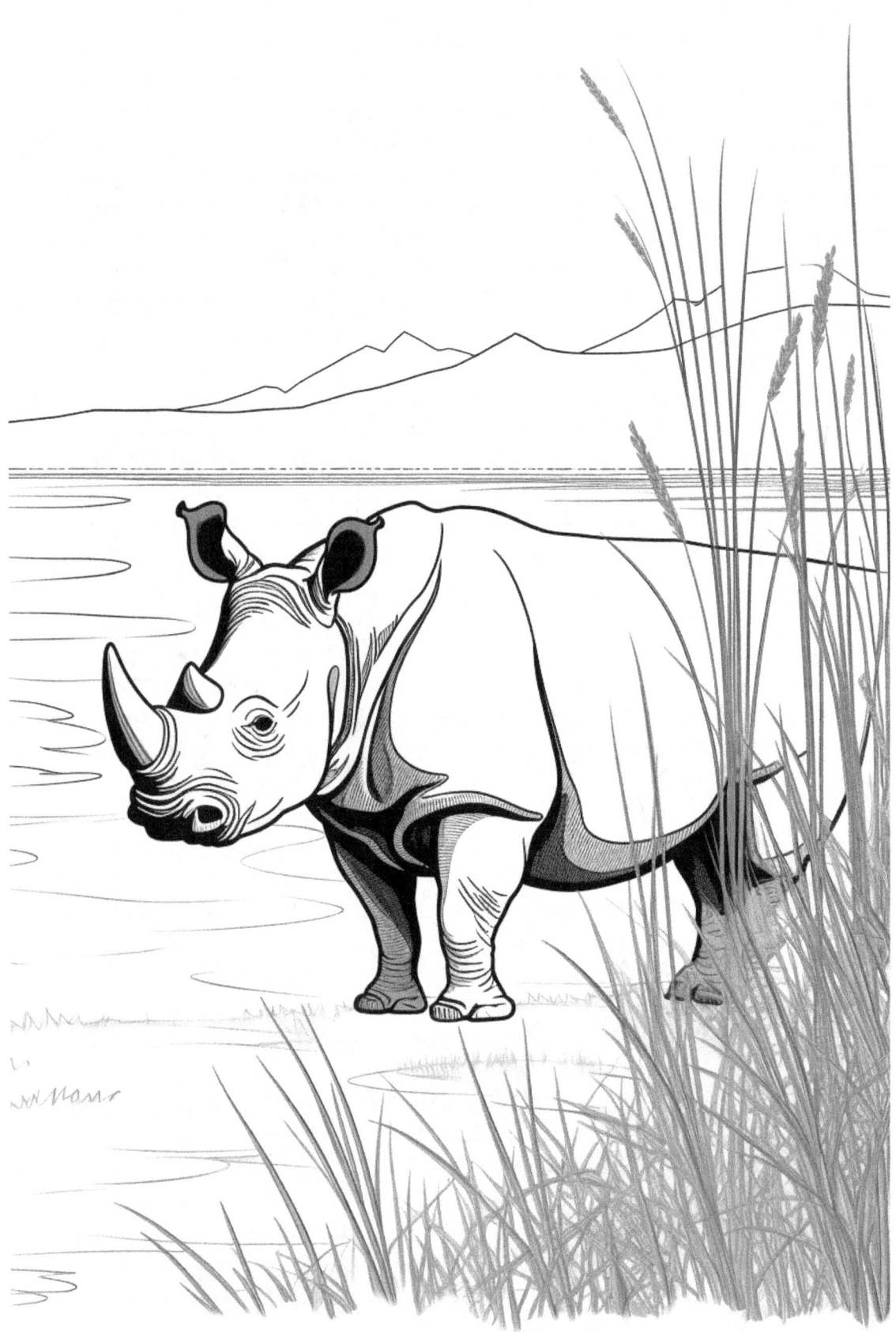

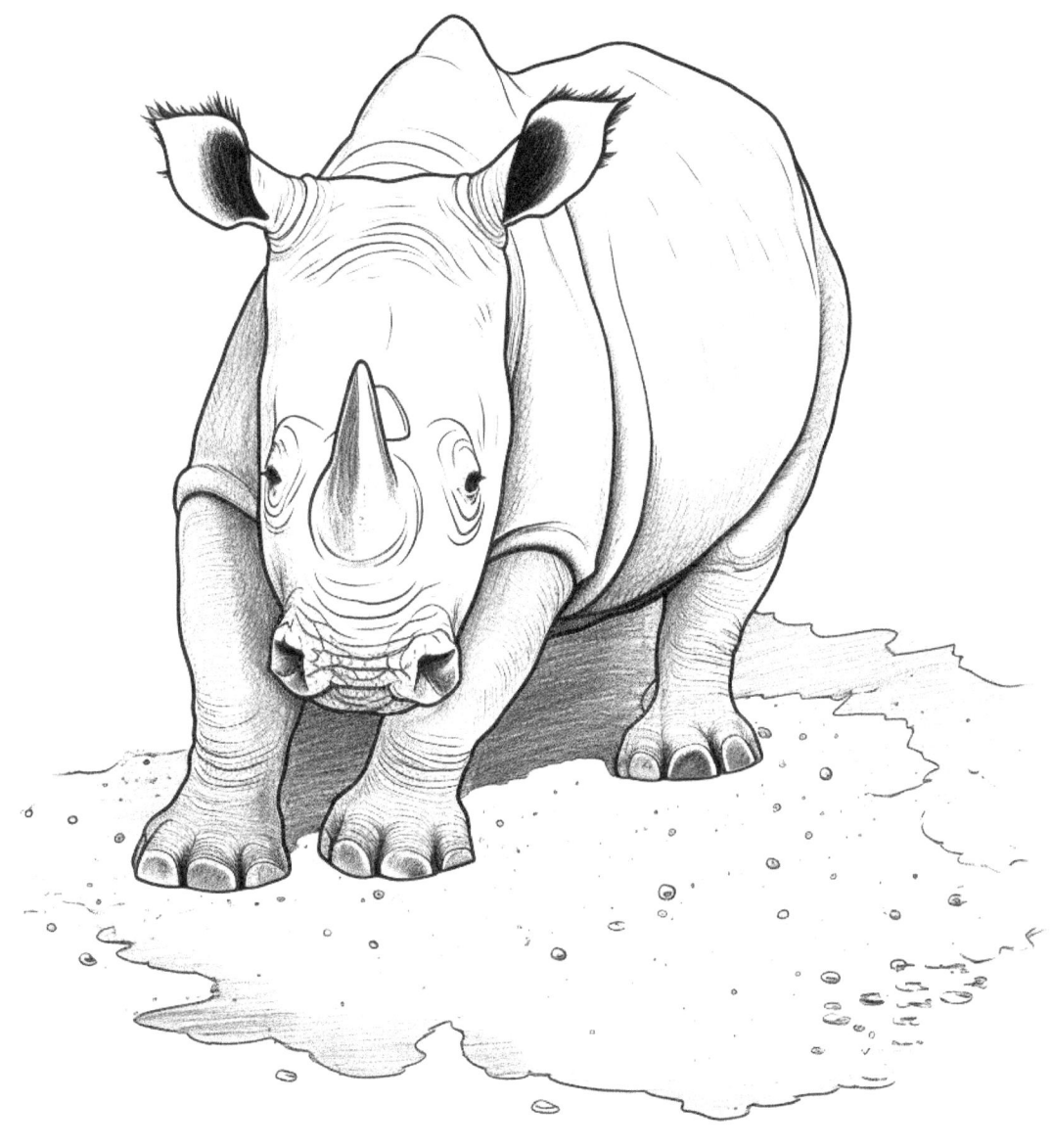

S is for Seal

In the frigid waters of the Arctic, the seal glides, and dives,

With their flippers and blubber, they're a creature that thrives.

They're carnivores that eat fish, squid, and some krill,

And with their streamlined hunter bodies, their belly is easy to fill.

Seals often bask on ice floes, just waiting to swim when its time,

And with their stunning underwater displays, they're creatures that shine!

Seals are fascinating creatures, that's for sure,

And with their playful nature, we can't help but adore!

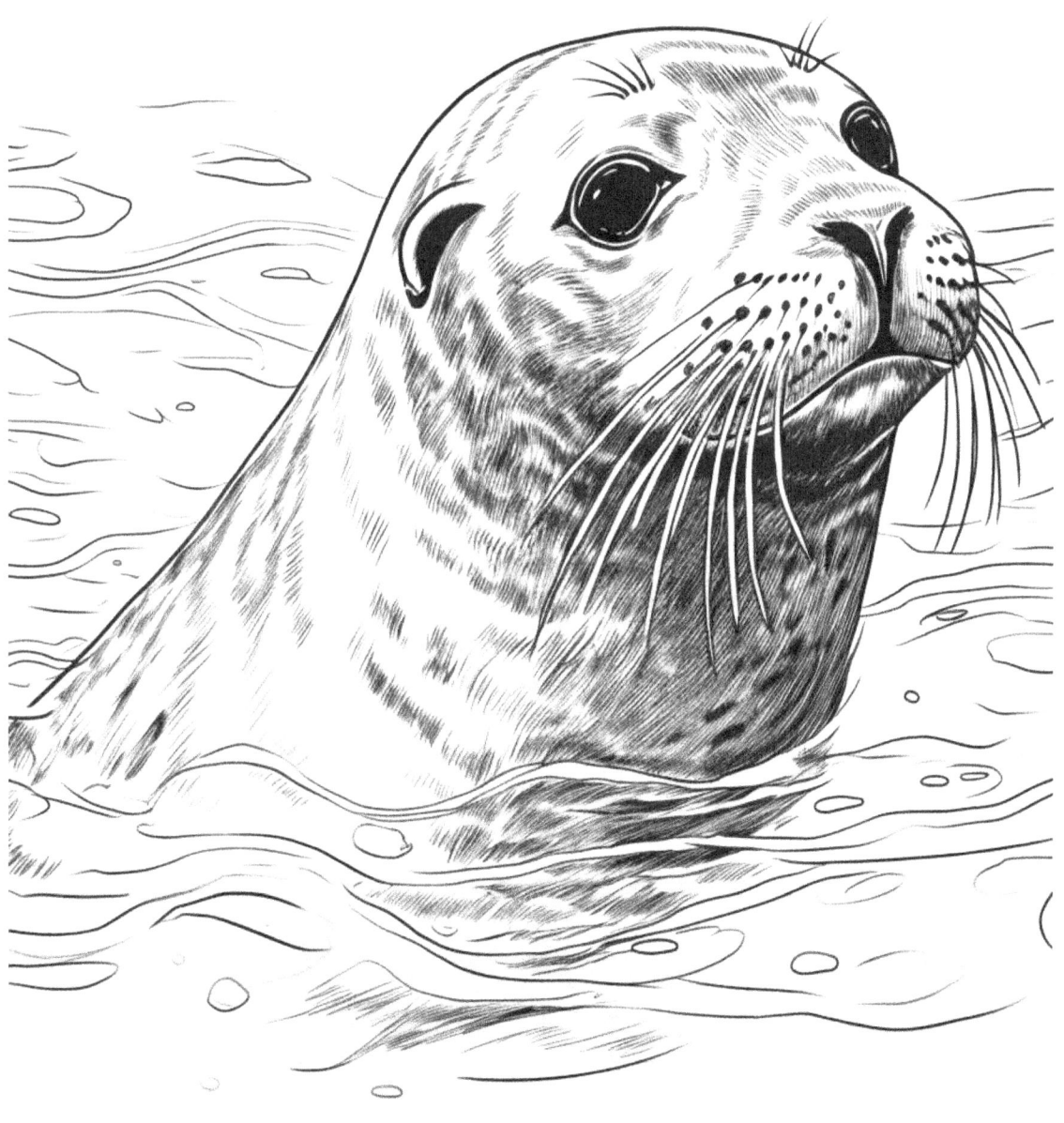

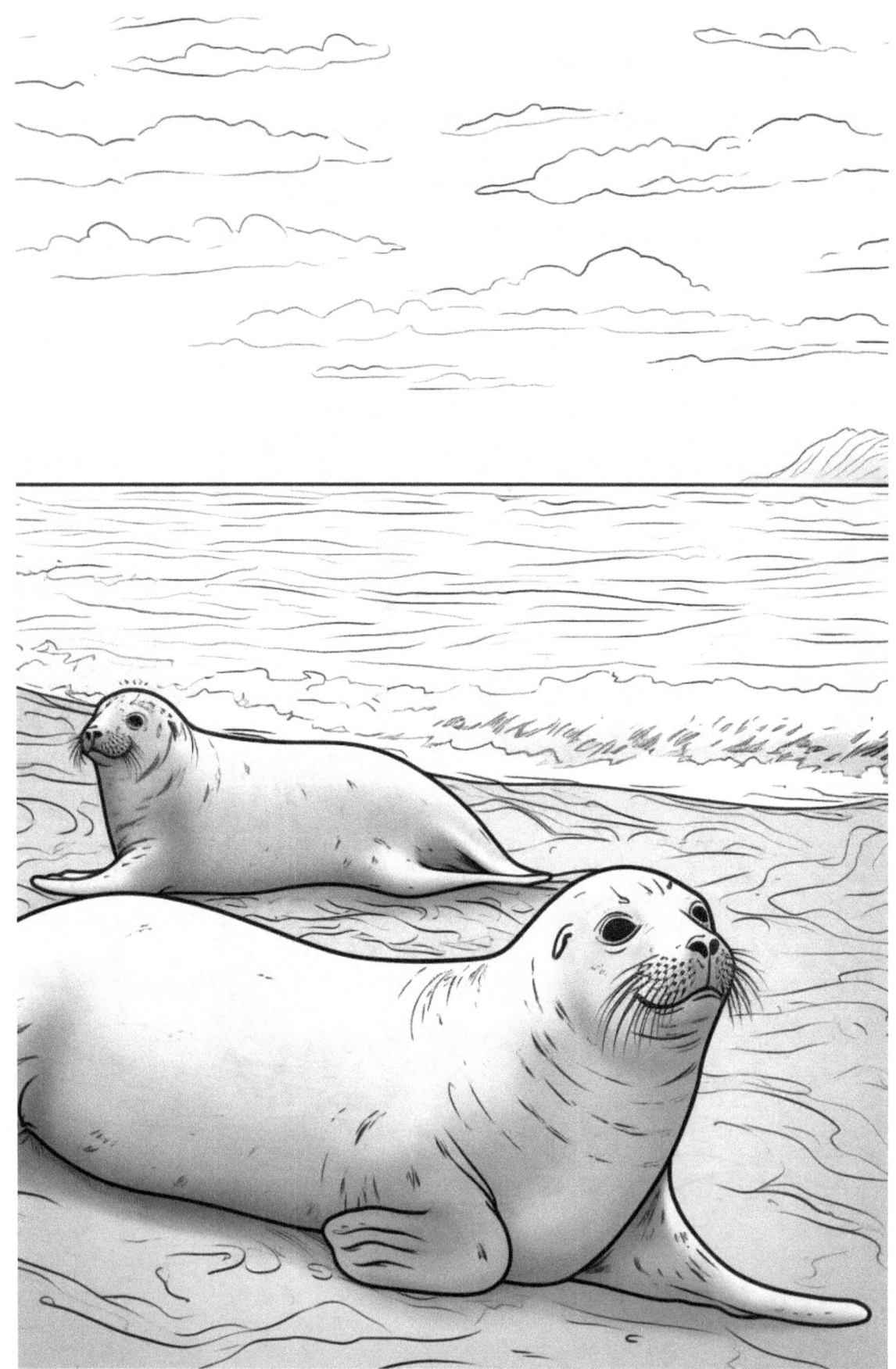

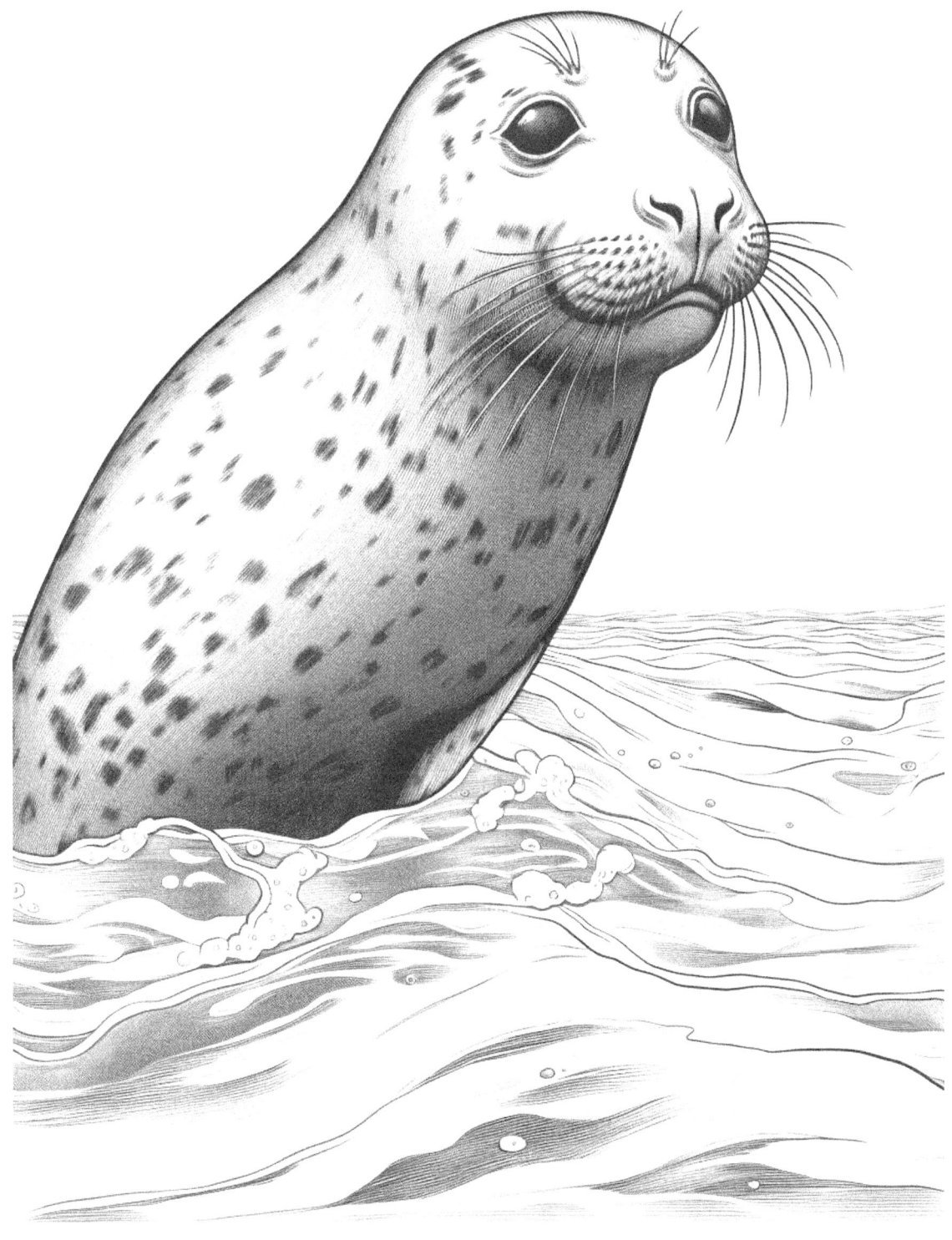

T is for Tiger

These majestic cats are skilled swimmers, able to cross rivers wide,

And with their markings camouflaging, they're not hard to hide.

They're carnivores that eat deer, wild pigs, and more,

And with their solitary habits, they love to go and explore.

Though they are solitary animals, tigers communicate through calls,

And with their social bonds, they build connections with others, not put-up walls.

Let's appreciate these amazing cats, with their strength and their grace,

A tiger is an incredible creature, worth learning to embrace.

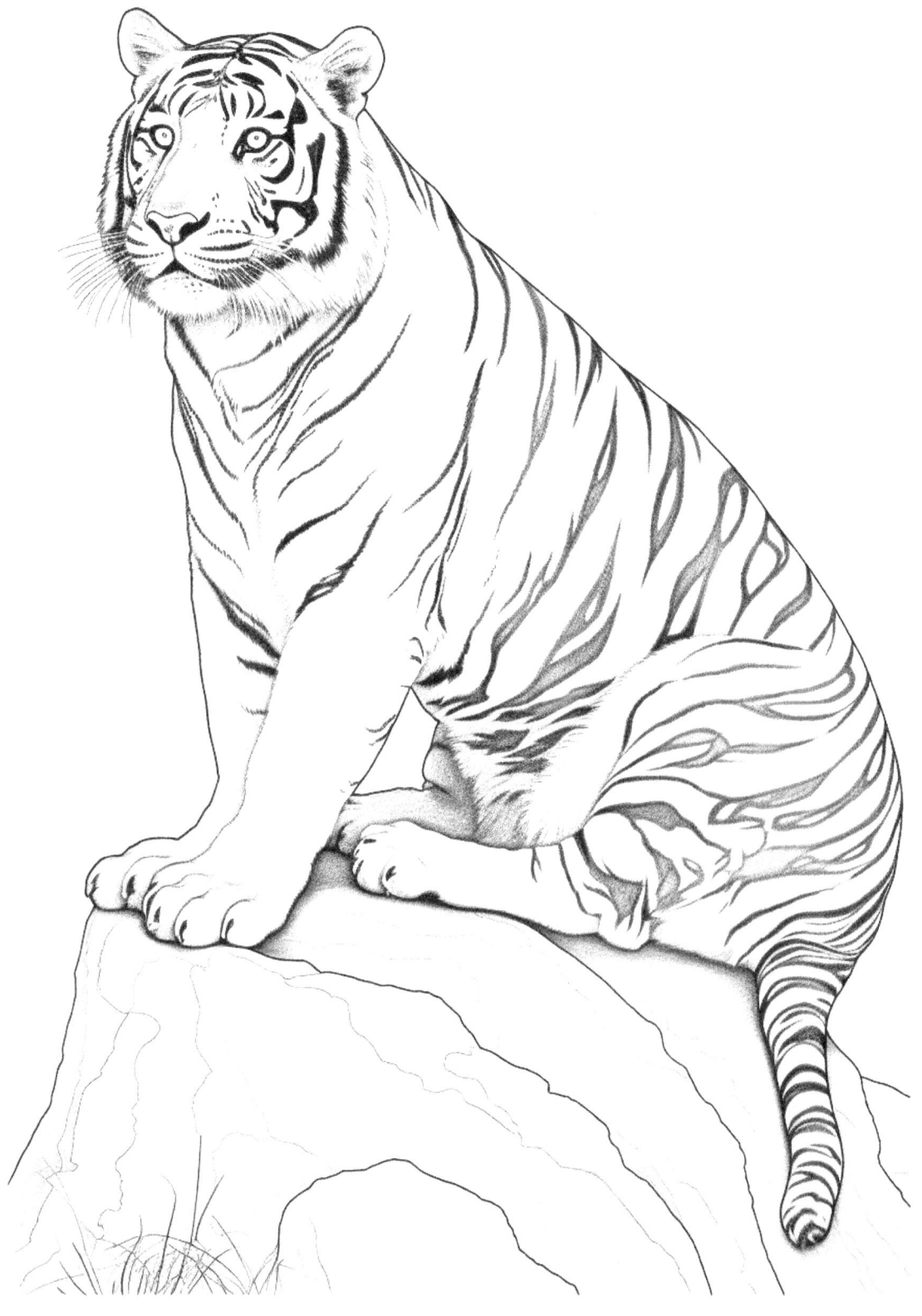

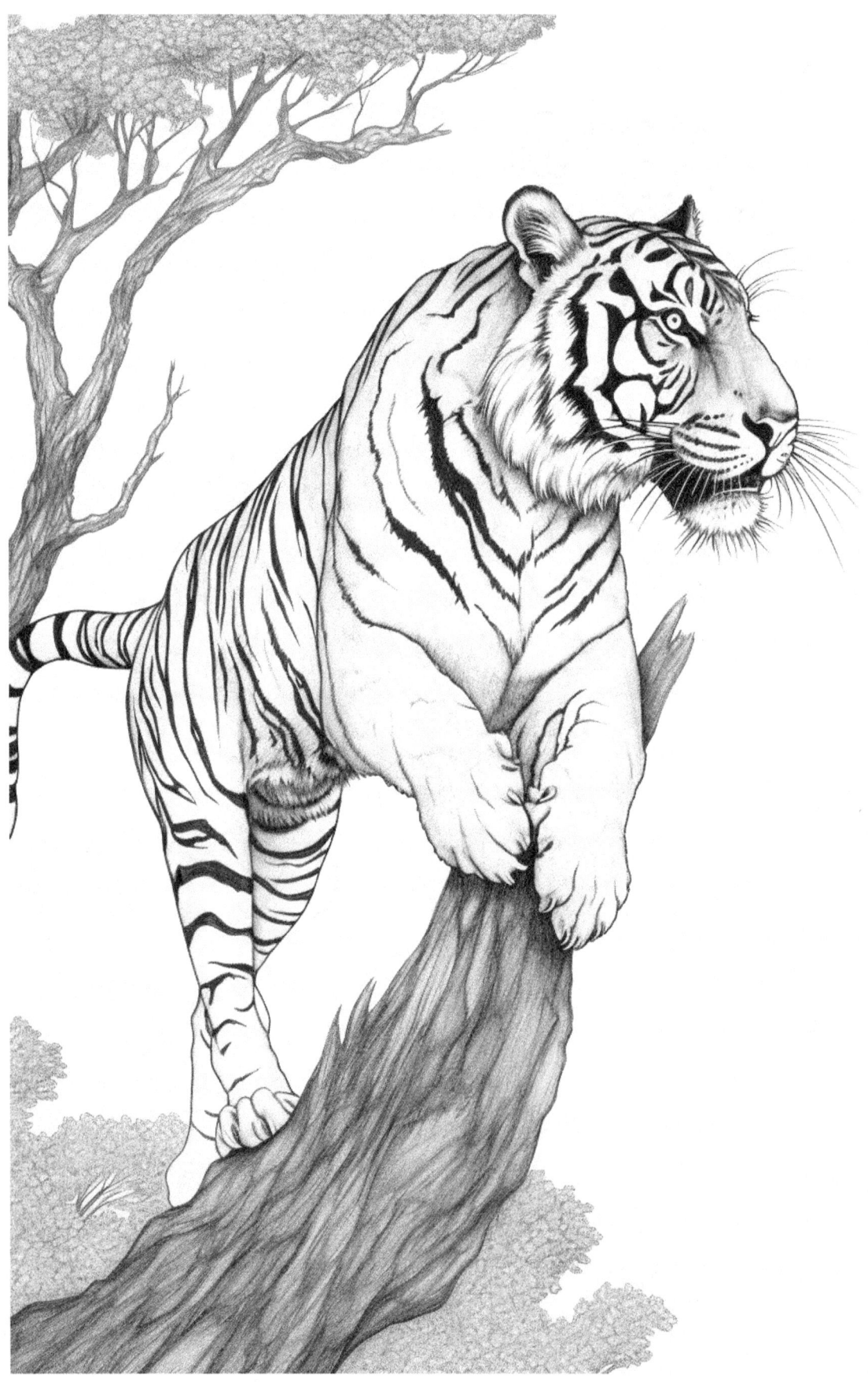

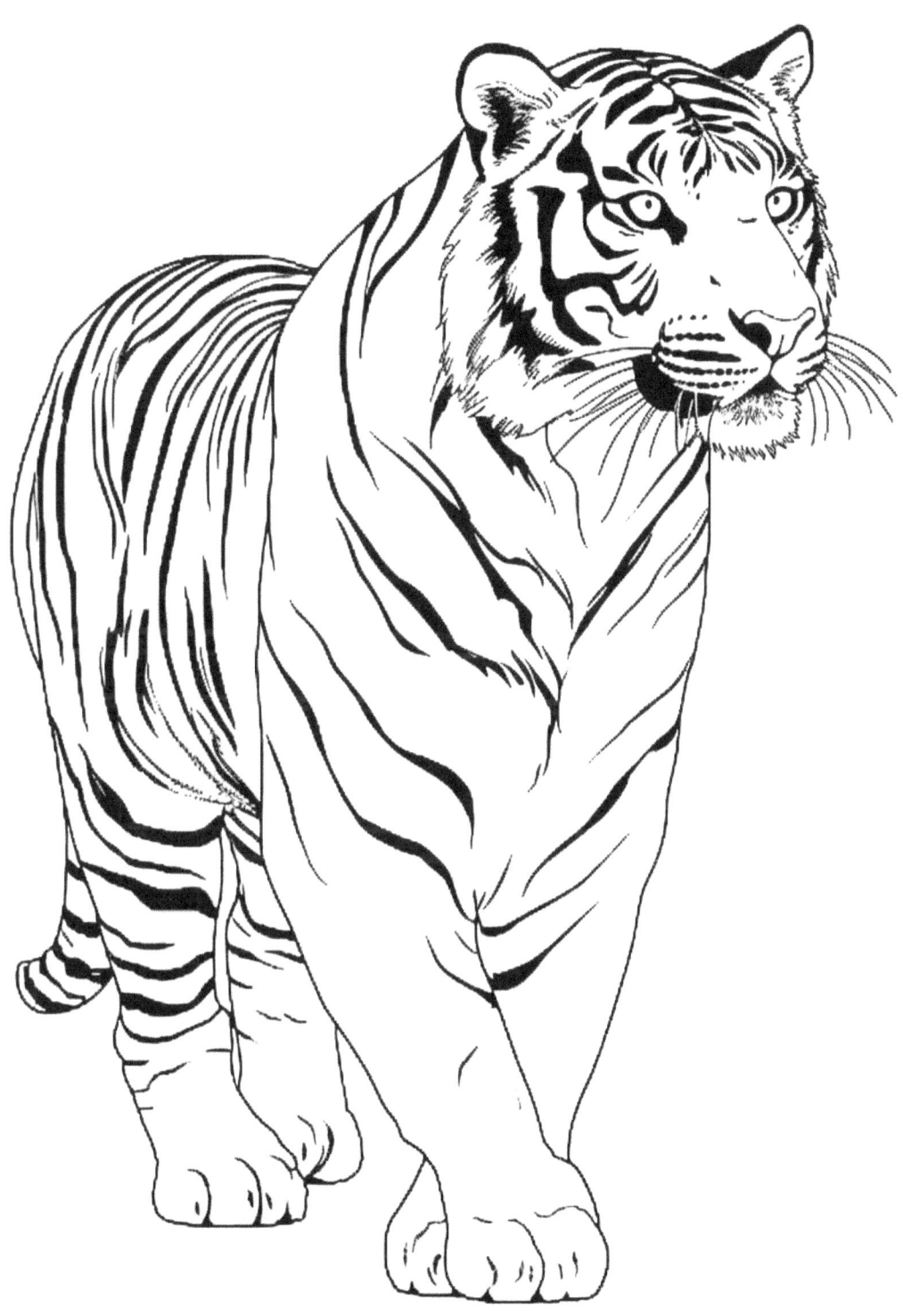

U is for Urial

In the cold and steep mountains of Asia, the Urial grazes and plays,

With their curly horns and woolly coat, they're creatures that tend to amaze.

They're nimble climbers that leap deep stone gaps with ease,

And with their keen eyesight and balance they're sure climbing is sure to please.

Their herds are led by the most experienced female,

And with their complicated social bonds, it's an amazing detail.

Urials have adapted to the harshest environments with rugged terrain,

An animal whose life is so incredible, it's hard to explain.

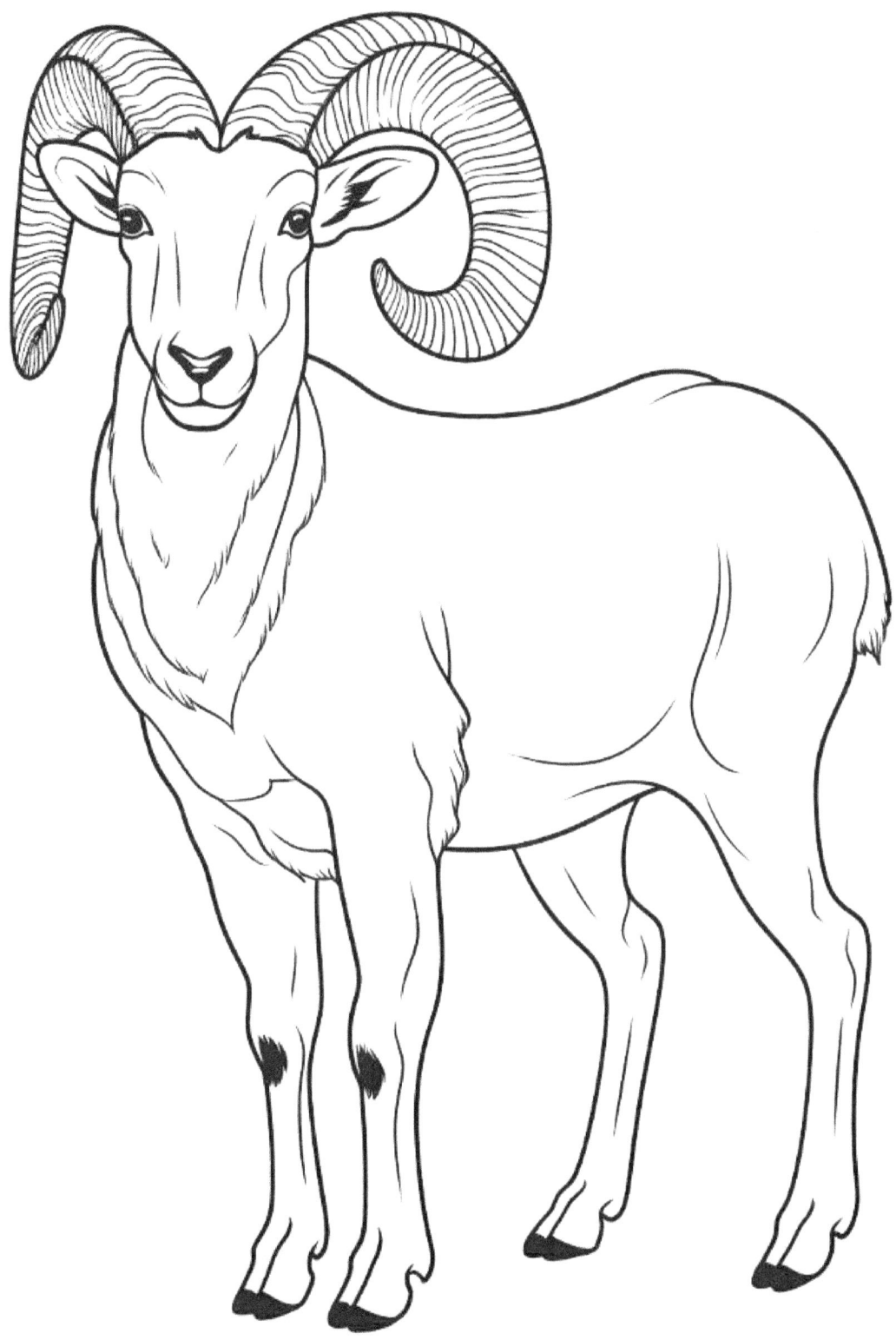

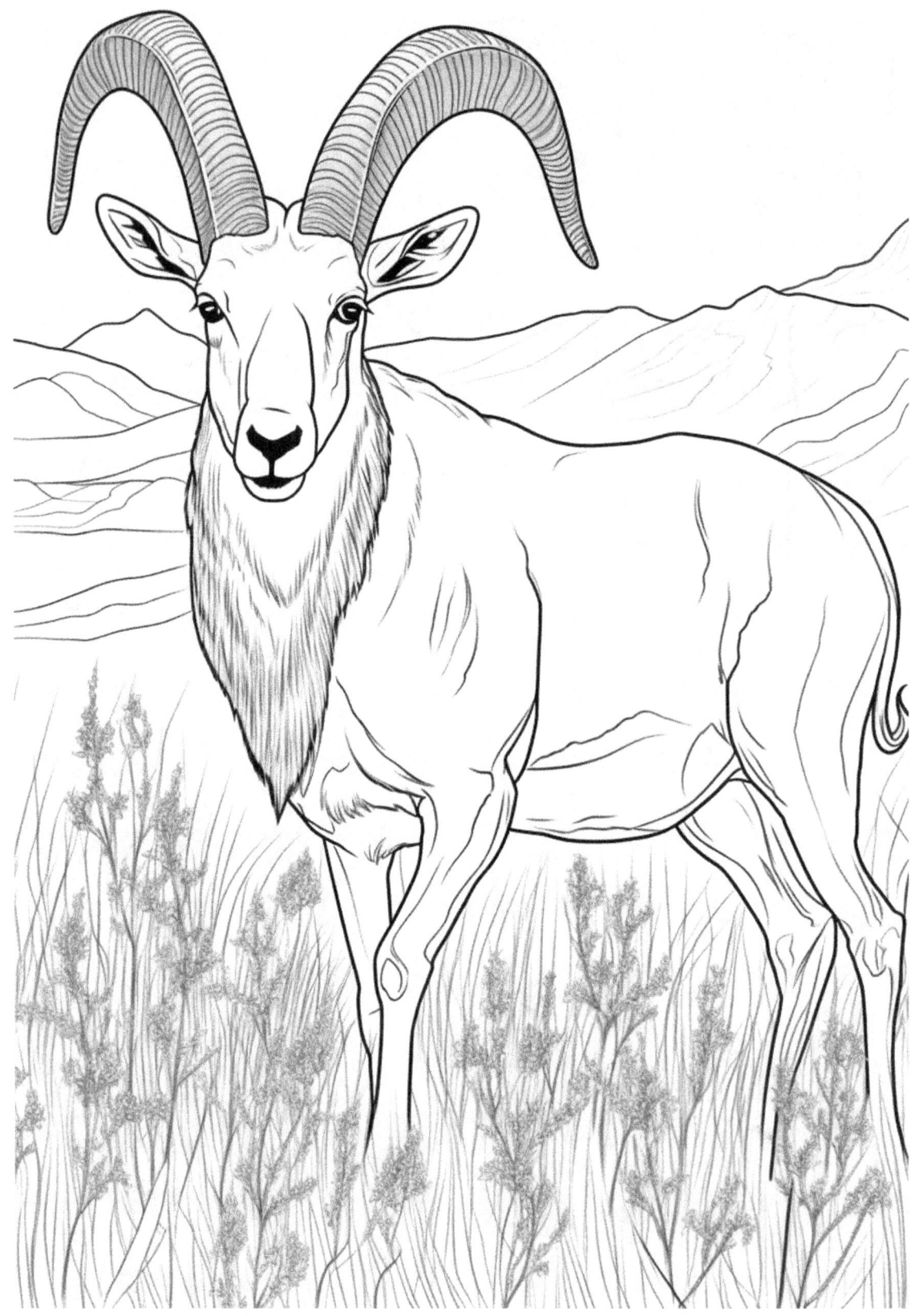

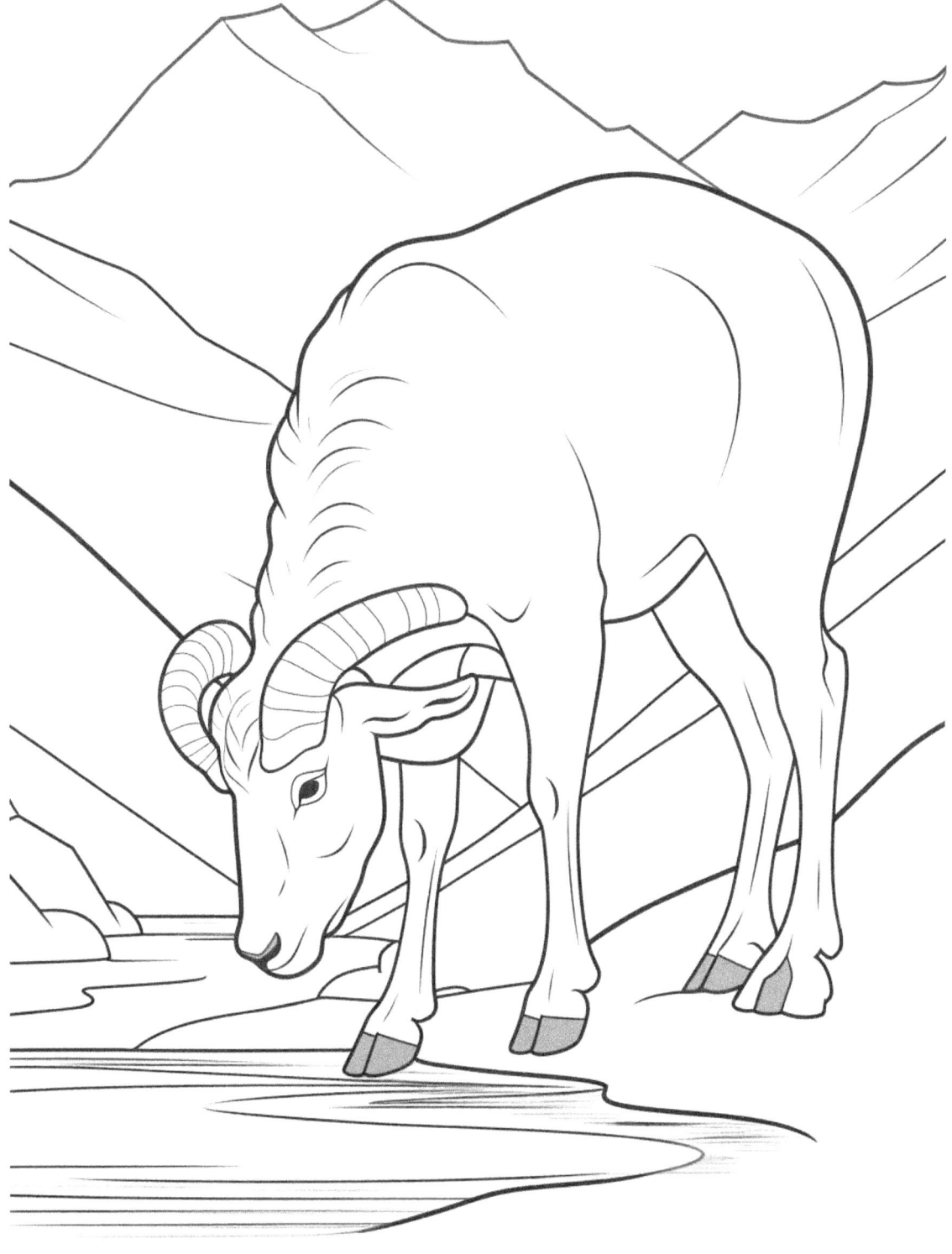

V is for Vulture

High in the sky vultures do soar on wings that are wide,

They are great birds of prey, with a scavenger's pride.

They help keep our planet clean, by eating up the dead,

Their sharp eyes and keen smell help them find food up ahead.

Their bald heads may seem strange, but it serves a special task,

To keep them clean while feasting, without wearing a messy mask.

These mighty birds may not be cute, but they're important to our world,

Vultures are fascinating creatures, with feathers tightly unfurled.

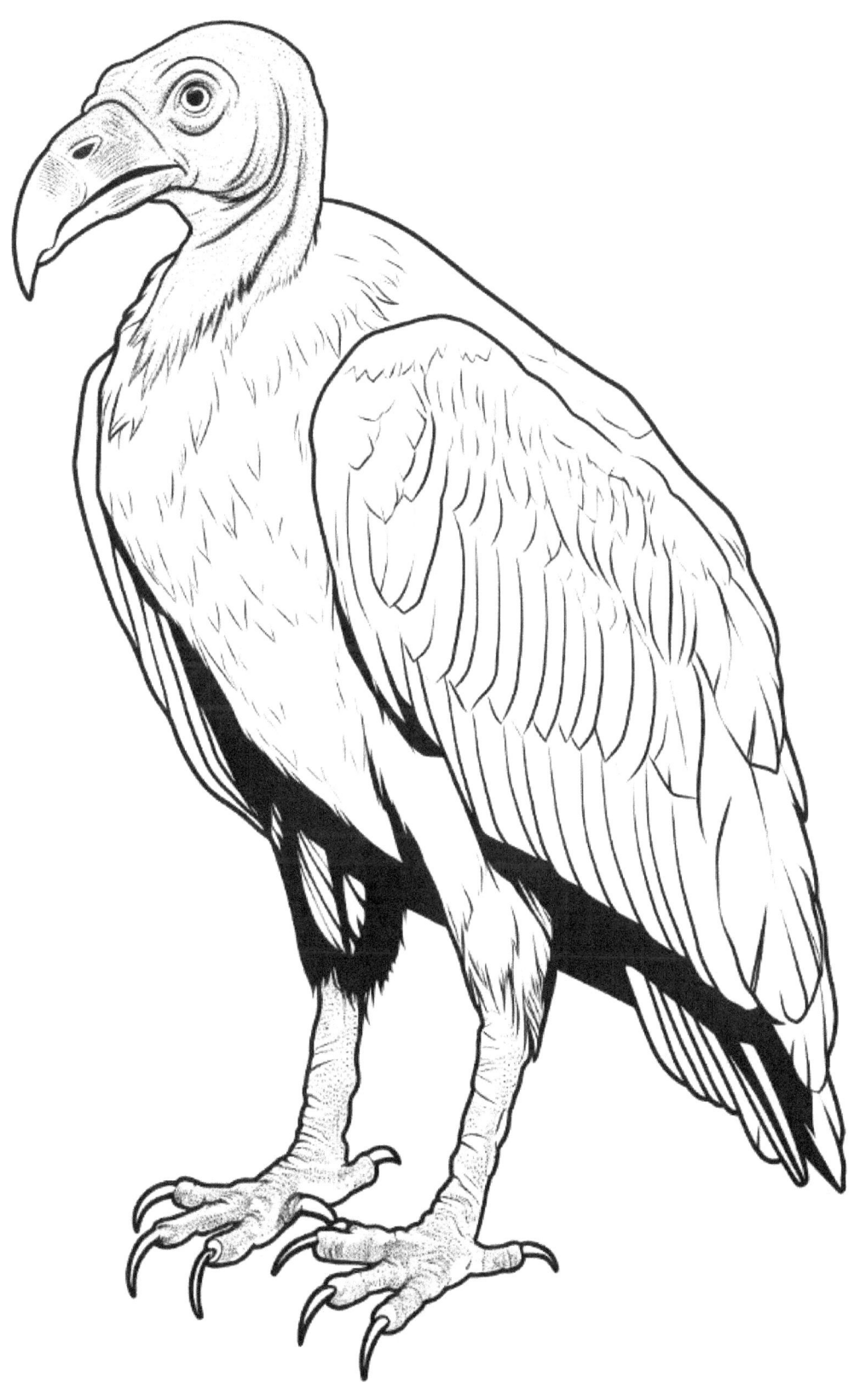

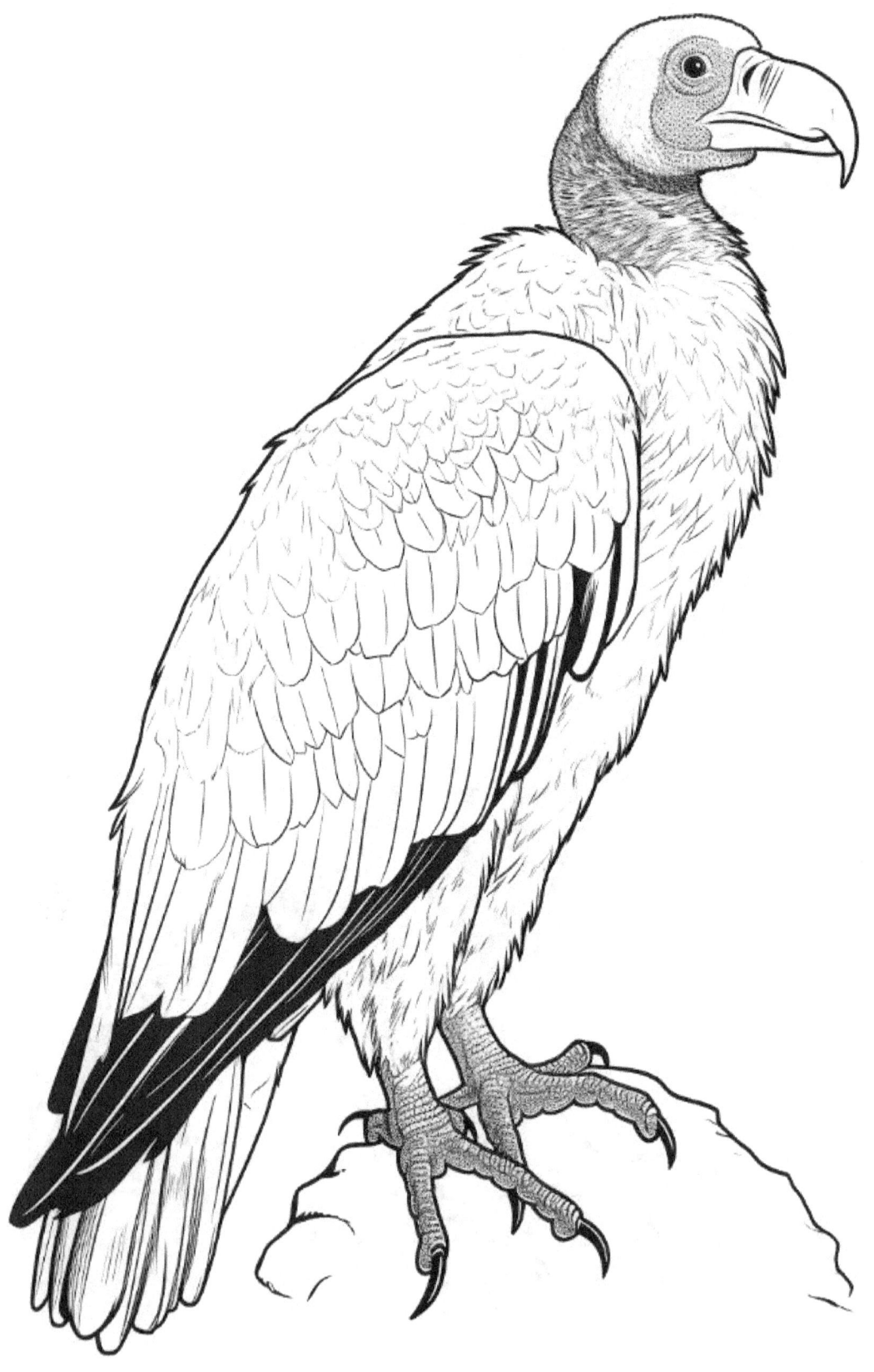

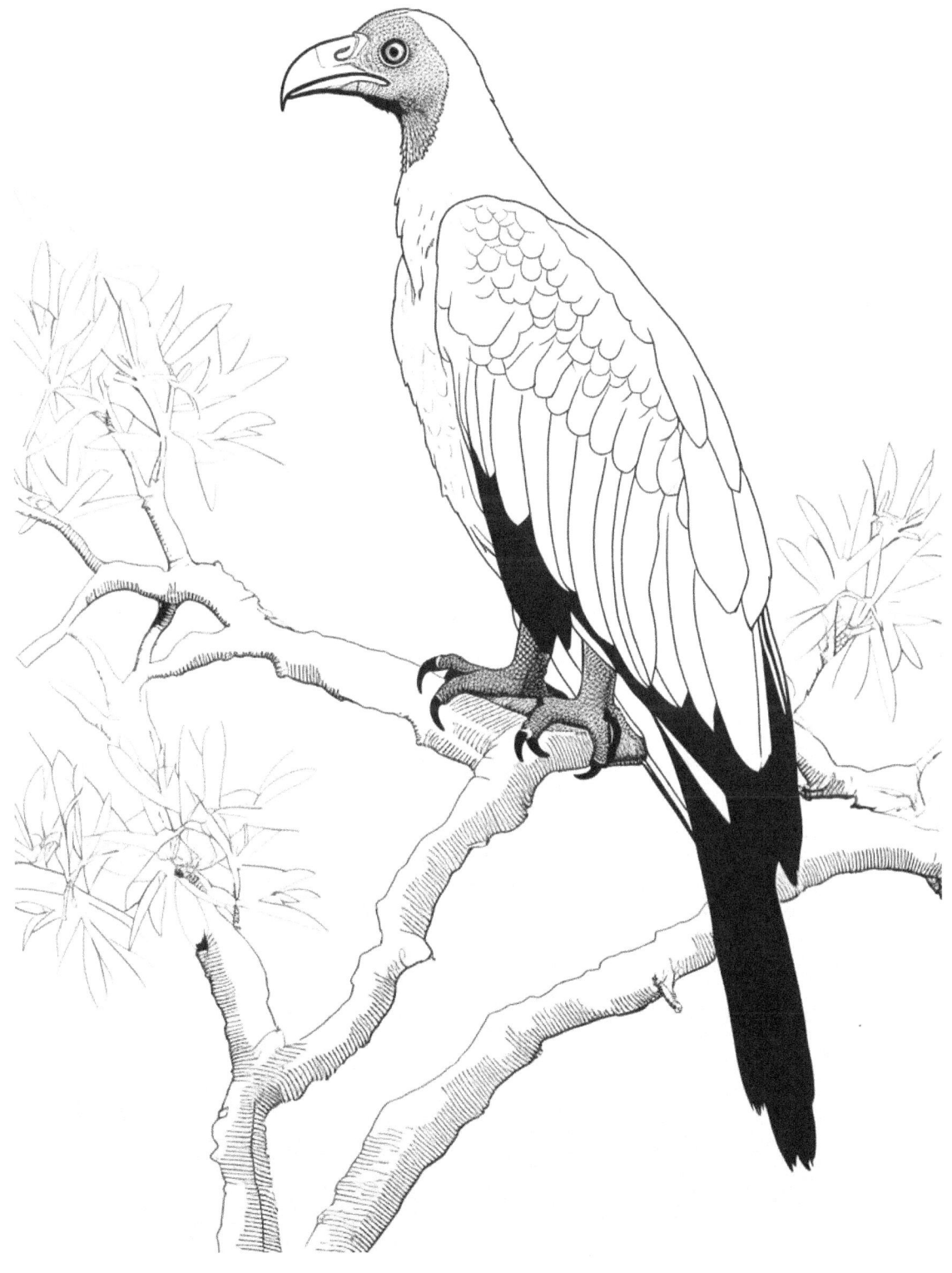

W is for Whale

In the worlds vast oceans, the whale swims a true creature of the sea,

With their massive size and melodic sounds, they're creatures that roam far and free.

They're filter feeders that eat krill and small fish,

And with their big baleen plates to help, they always fill their dish.

Whales are known for their unique sad sounding songs, which can travel for miles,

And with their deep dives and playful jumping breaches, they're creatures that bring smiles.

Whales are intelligent creatures with complex social lives,

And with their travels across oceans, they now thrive and survive.

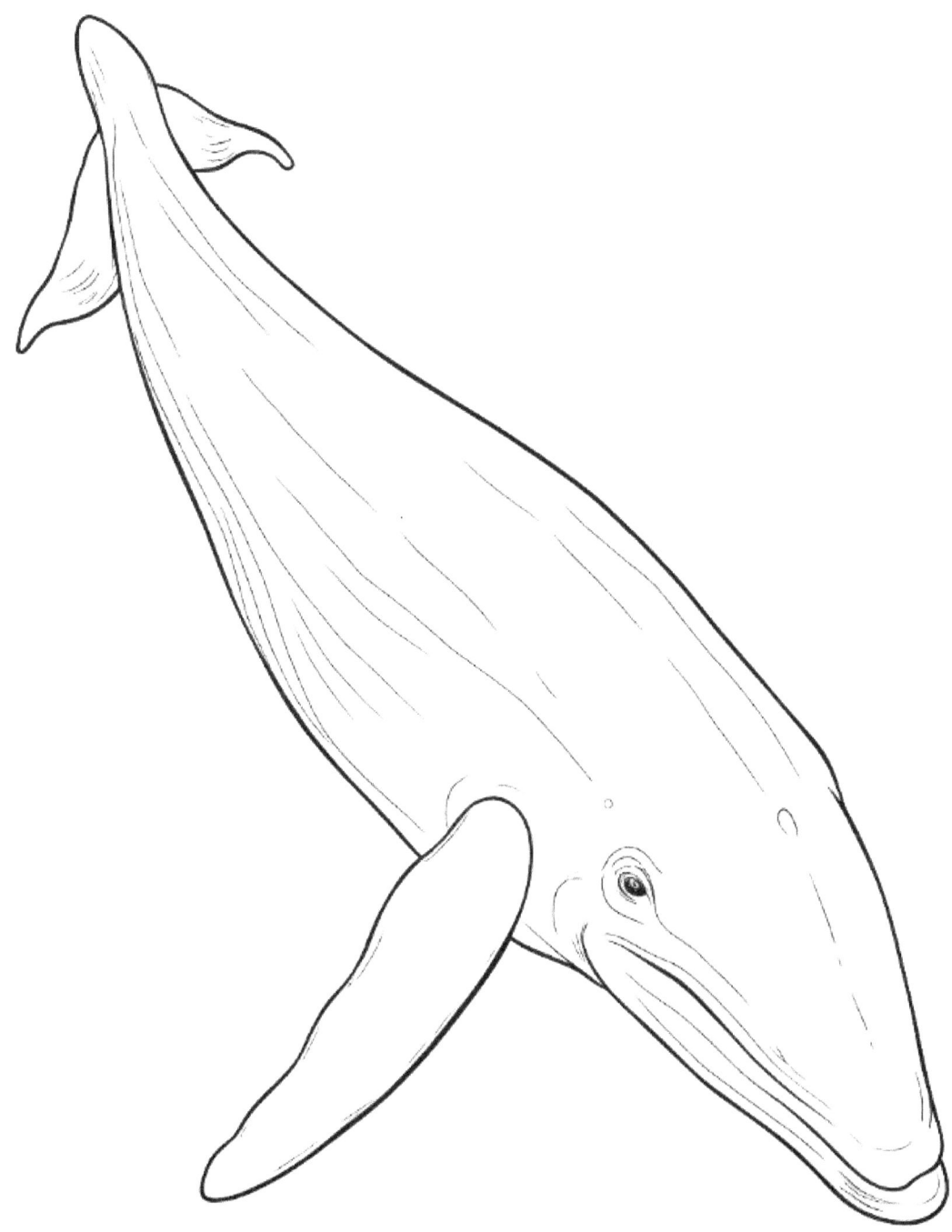

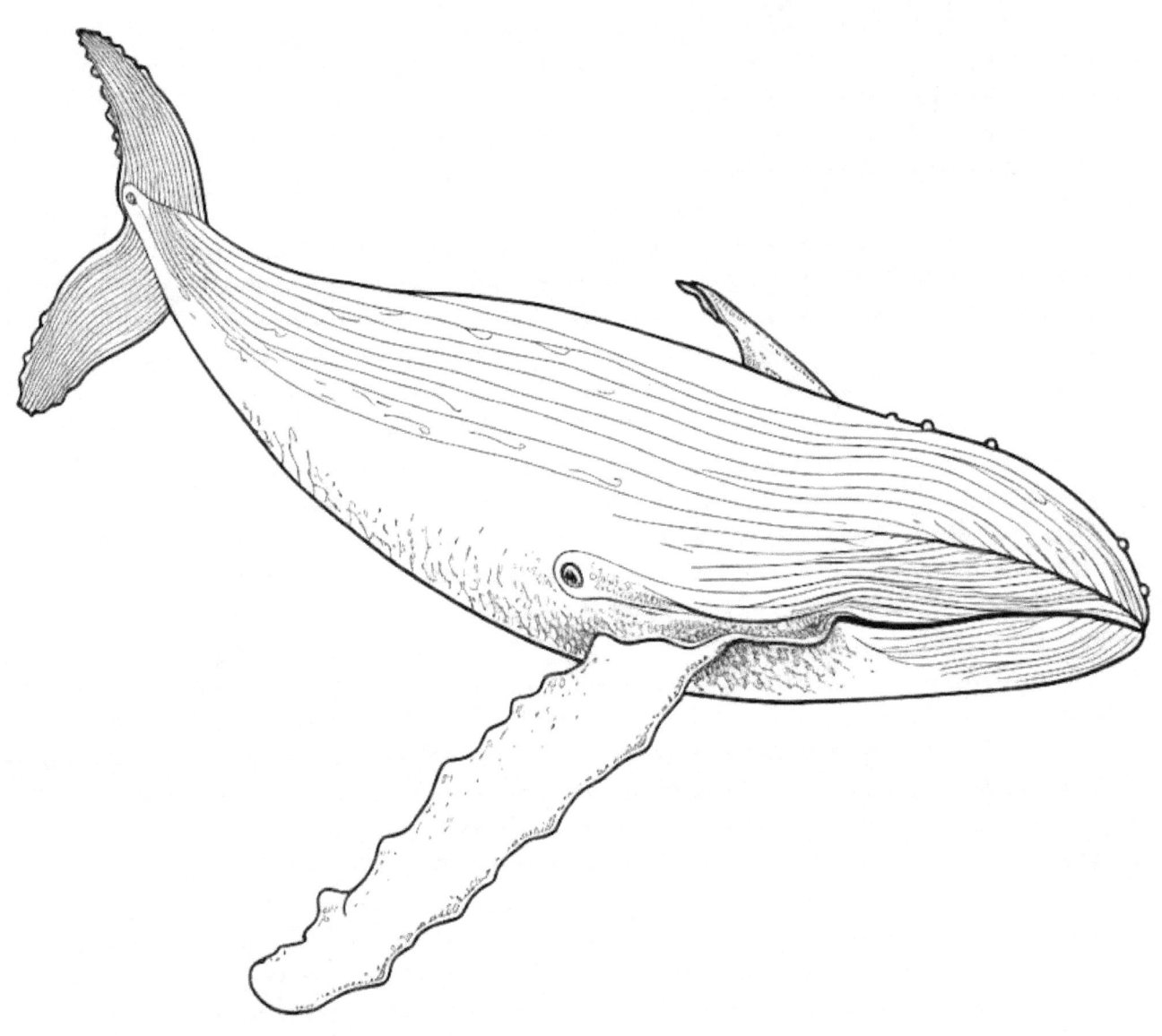

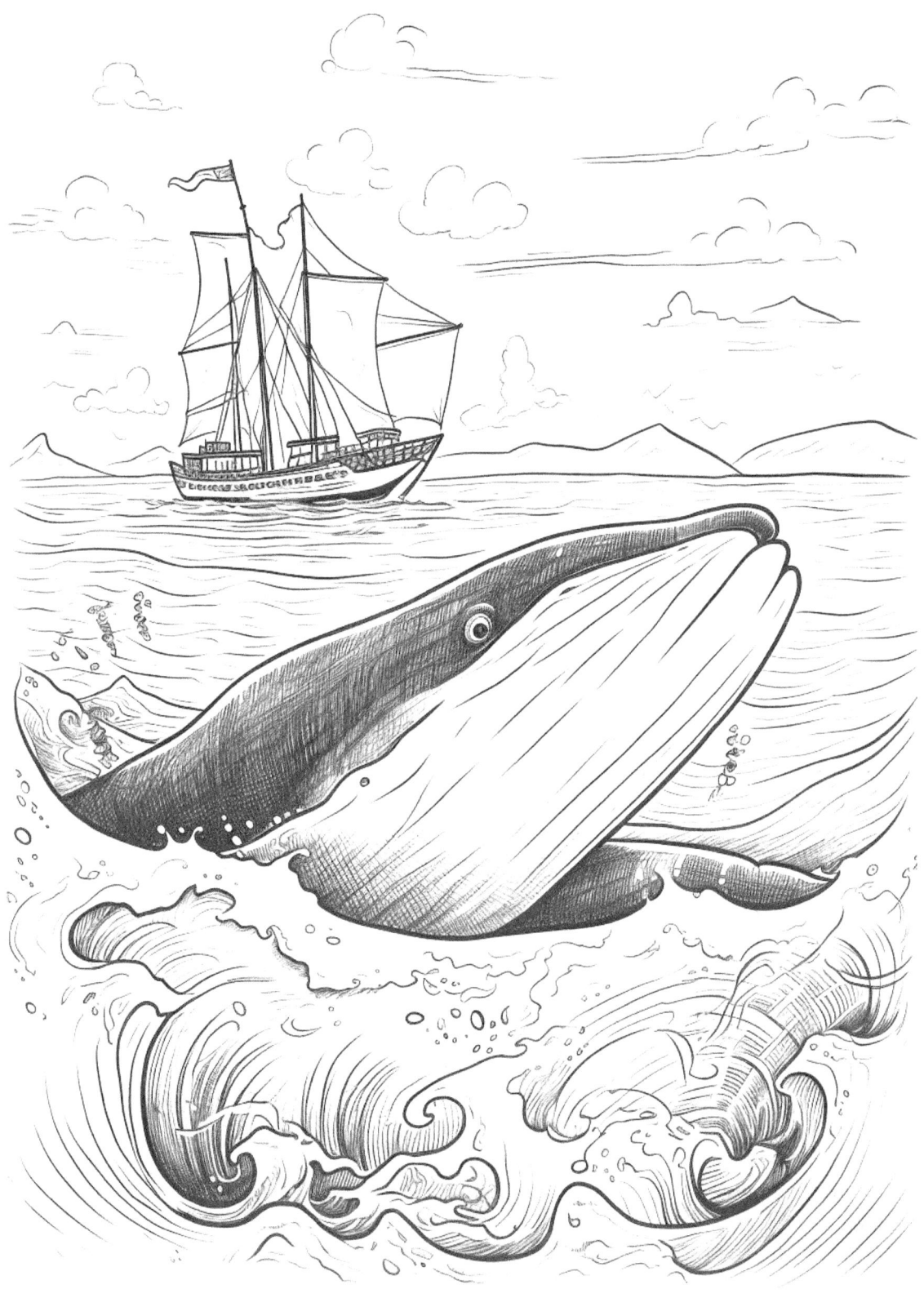

X is for Xenopus

In the muddy African streams, Xenopus thrives and plays,

With their slimy skin and tadpole grin, they brighten up our days.

Xenopus can also do something that's truly great,

If they lose a limb, they can grow it back, isn't that a cool trait?

Scientists love Xenopus for their unique biological facts,

And they study them to learn more about how regenerating tissues react.

In fact, their value to research in medicine has been so highly praised,

Making them ancient but fascinating creatures that still can amaze.

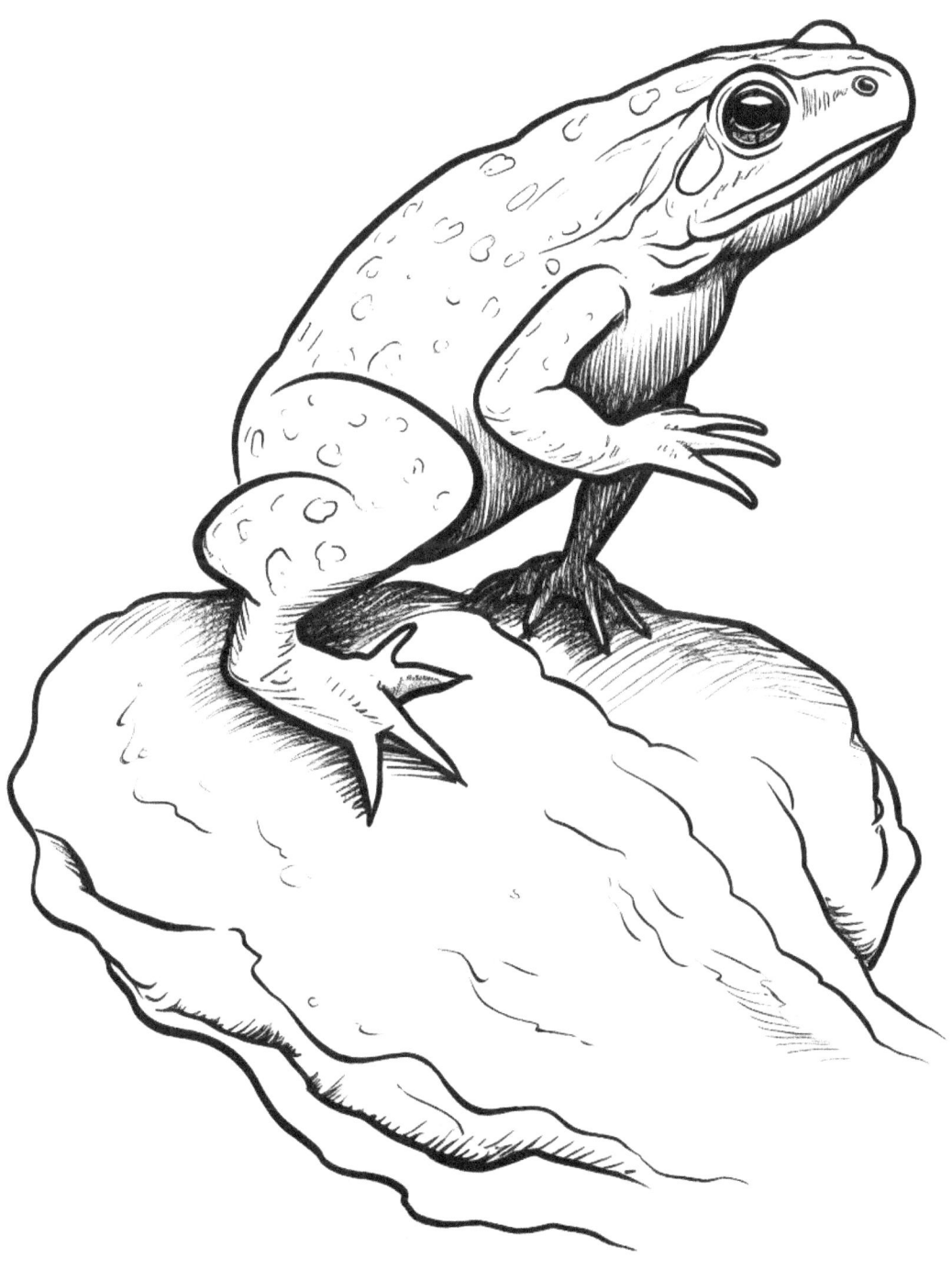

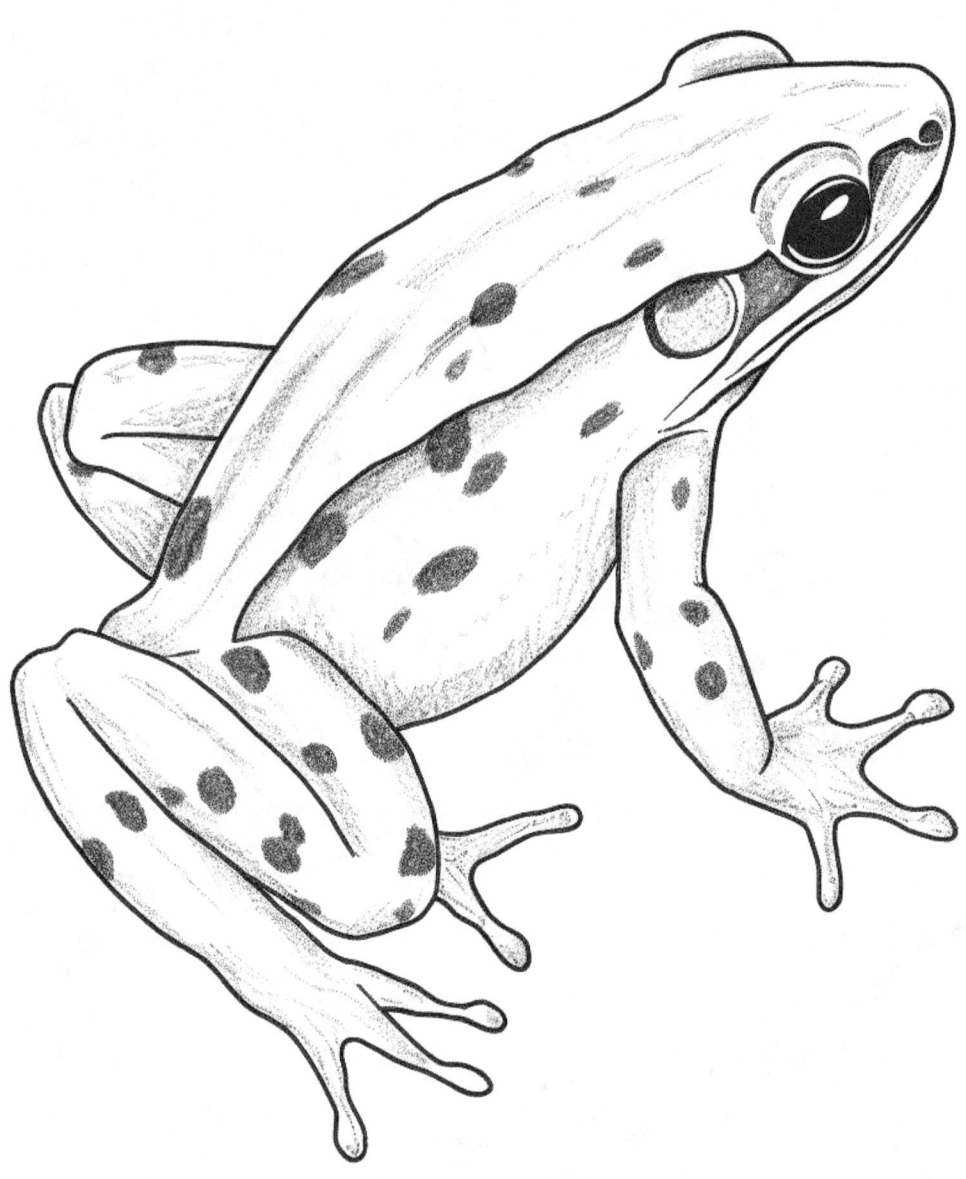

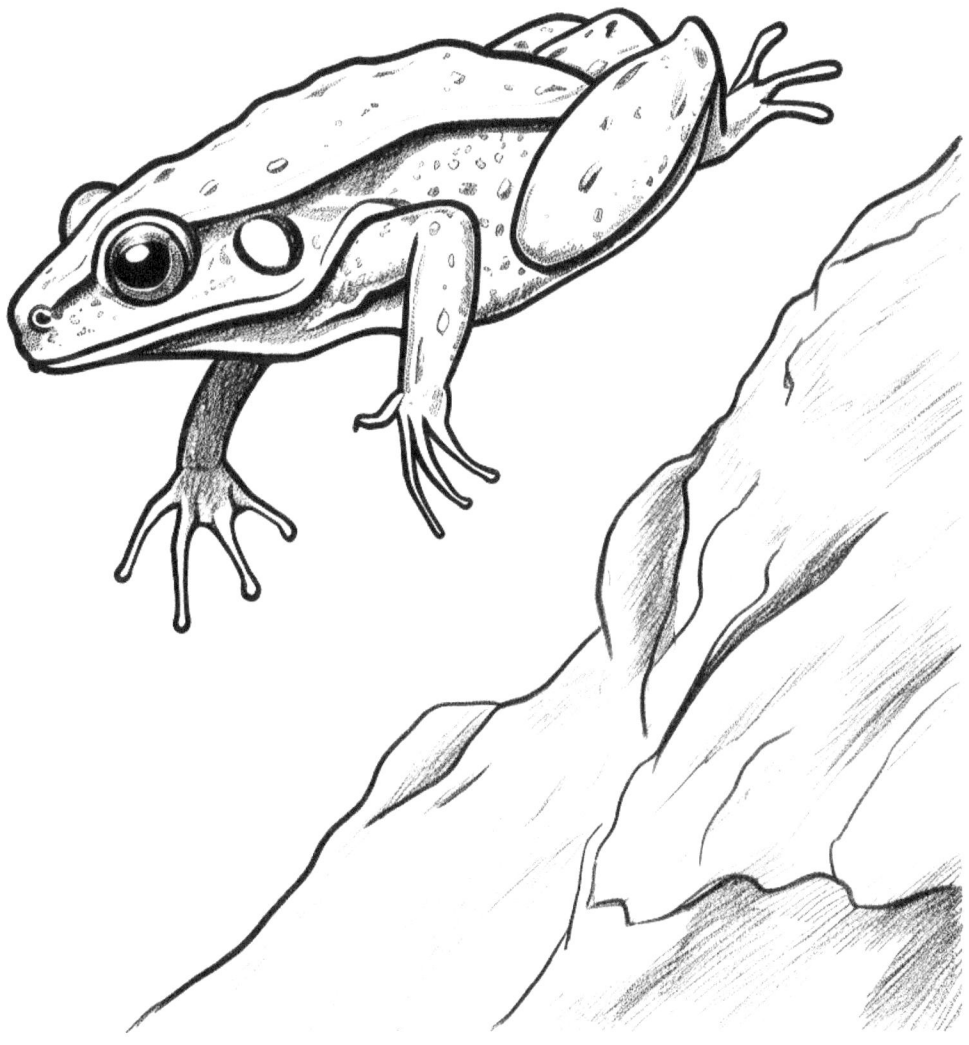

Y is for Yak

On the cold plateaus of Asia, the yak grazes, and trudges,

With thick necks and powerful horns, they're a creature that powerfully nudges.

From their thick shaggy wool, people make carpets and warm clothes,

And they're great for ploughing a farms field, as everyone knows.

With their kind friendly nature and childlike playful ways,

Yaks are sure to brighten up anyone's day!

Their thick fur keeps them cozy in the deep snow,

And their milk is rich, creamy, and will give you a healthy glow!

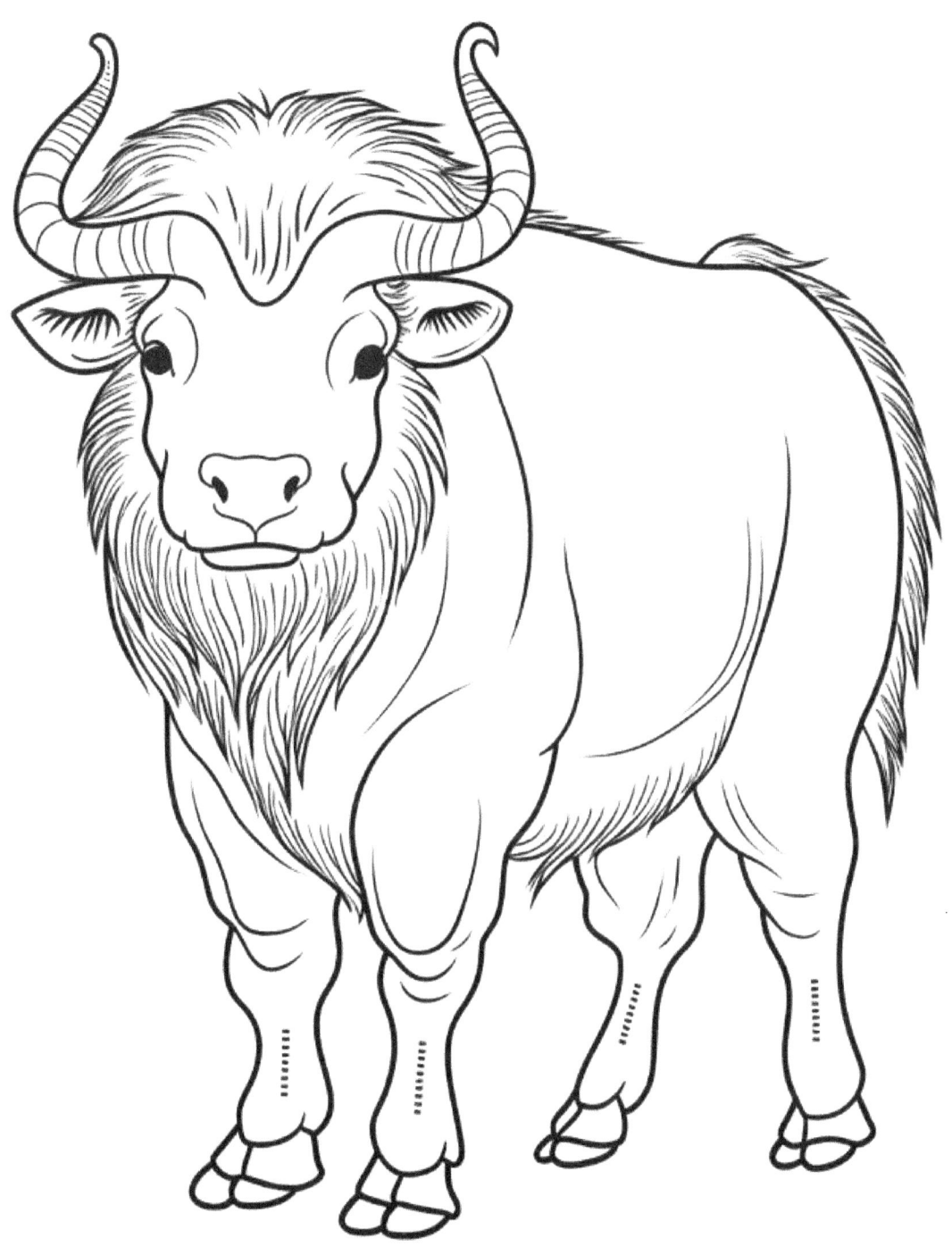

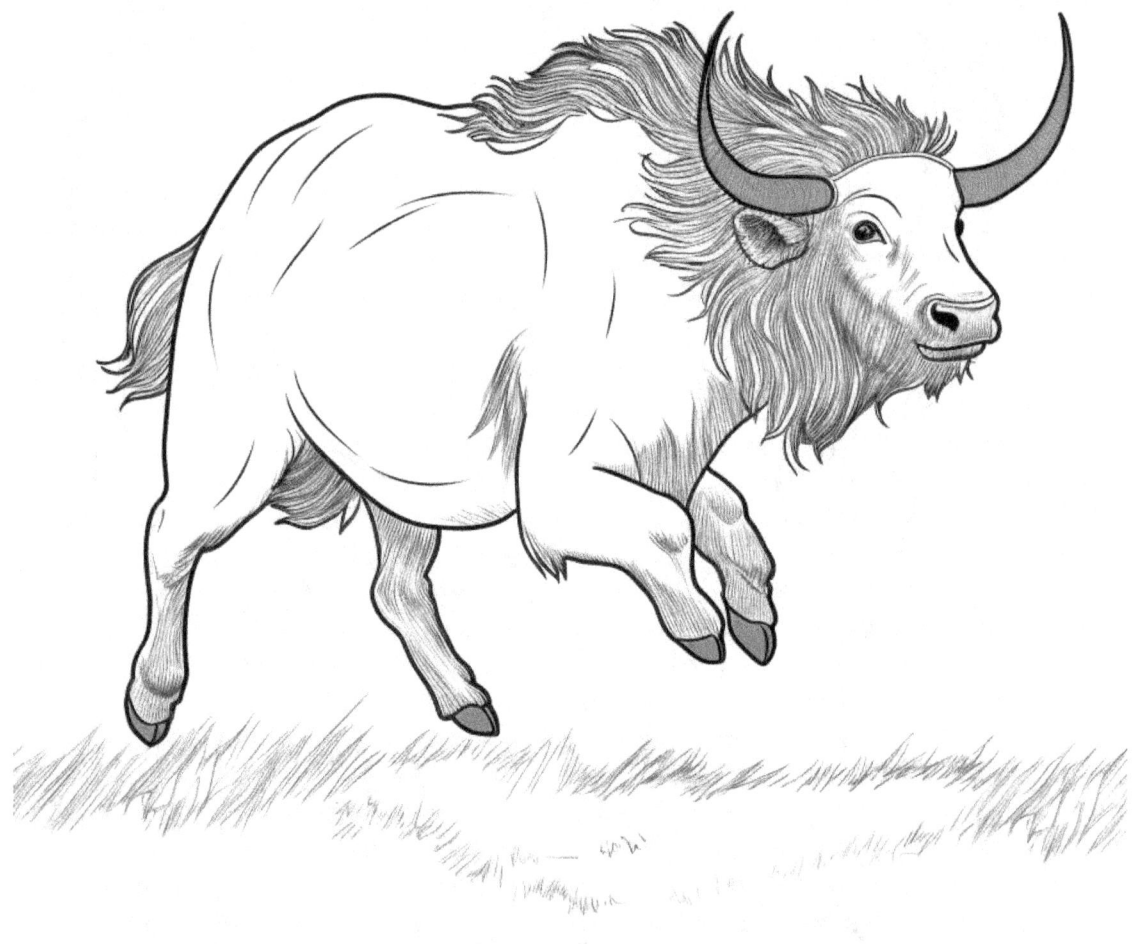

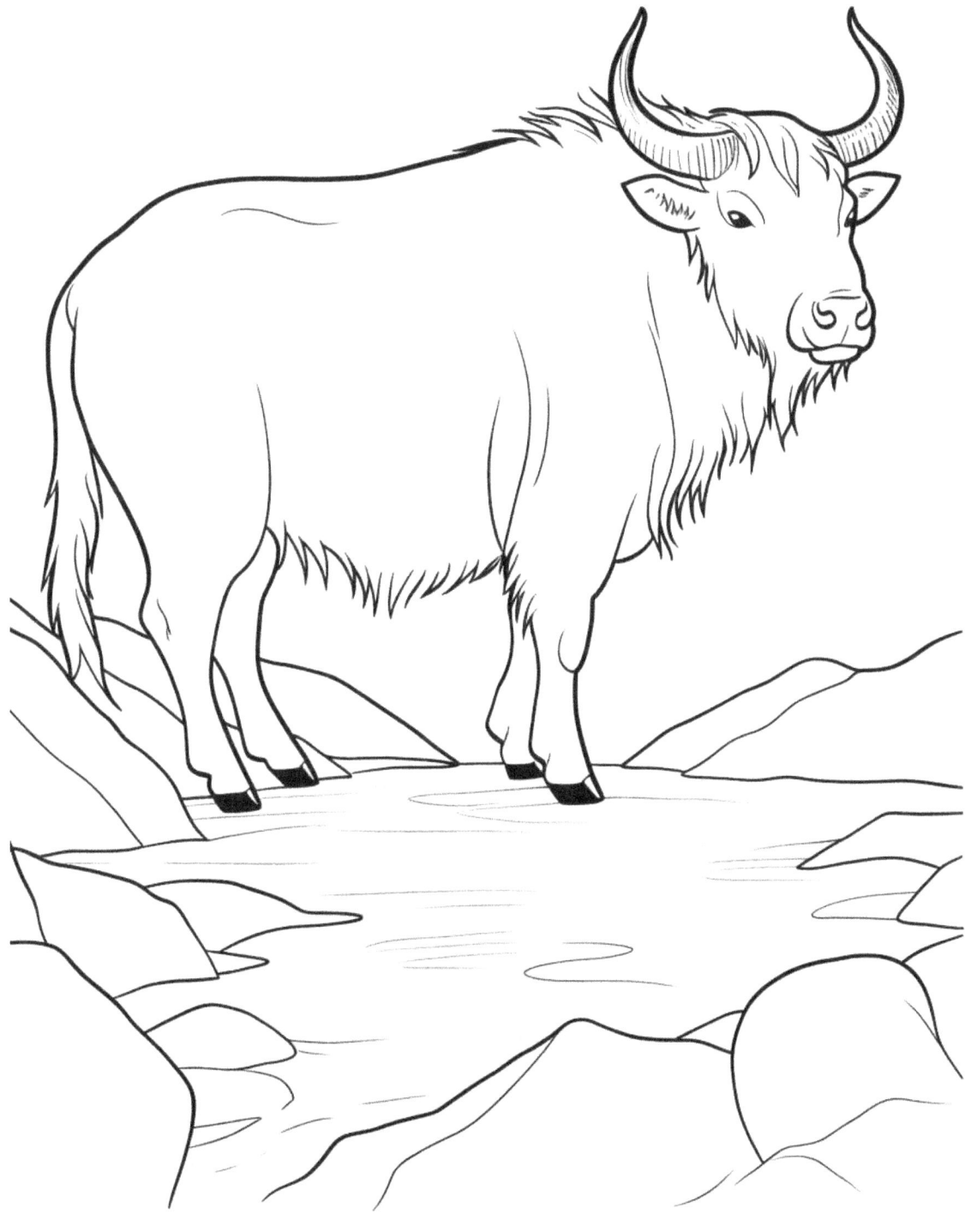

Z is for Zebra

They're grazers, munching on grass all day,

And with those long legs, they can quickly run away.

Their manes are like mohawks, short, spiky and standing up high,

With those big ears, they can hear something as small as a fly.

They're incredibly social animals, living in large family herds,

And their playful personalities are just simply absurd.

Let's appreciate these majestic creatures with happiness and zeal,

The world would be dull without the Zebra monochromatic appeal!

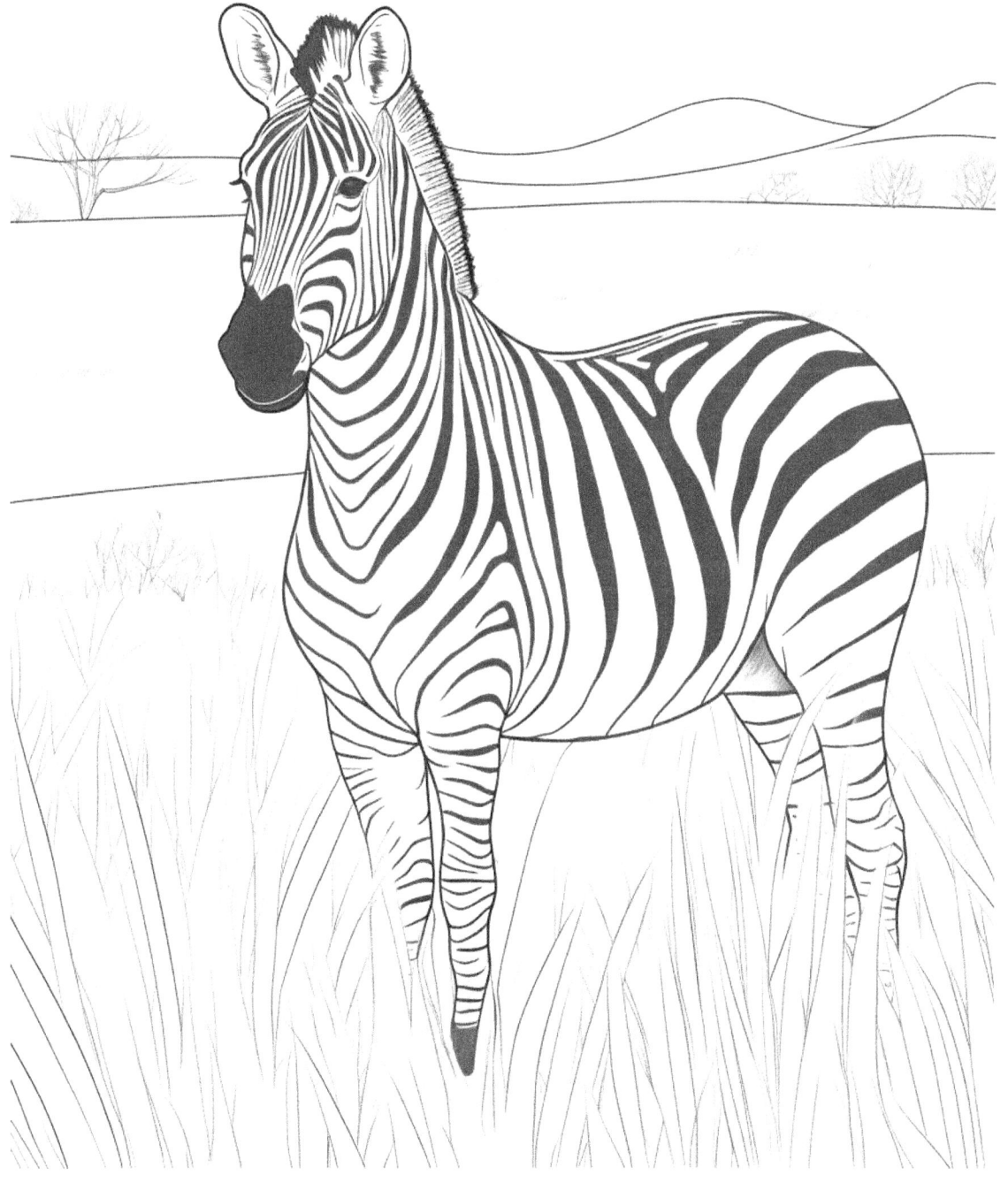

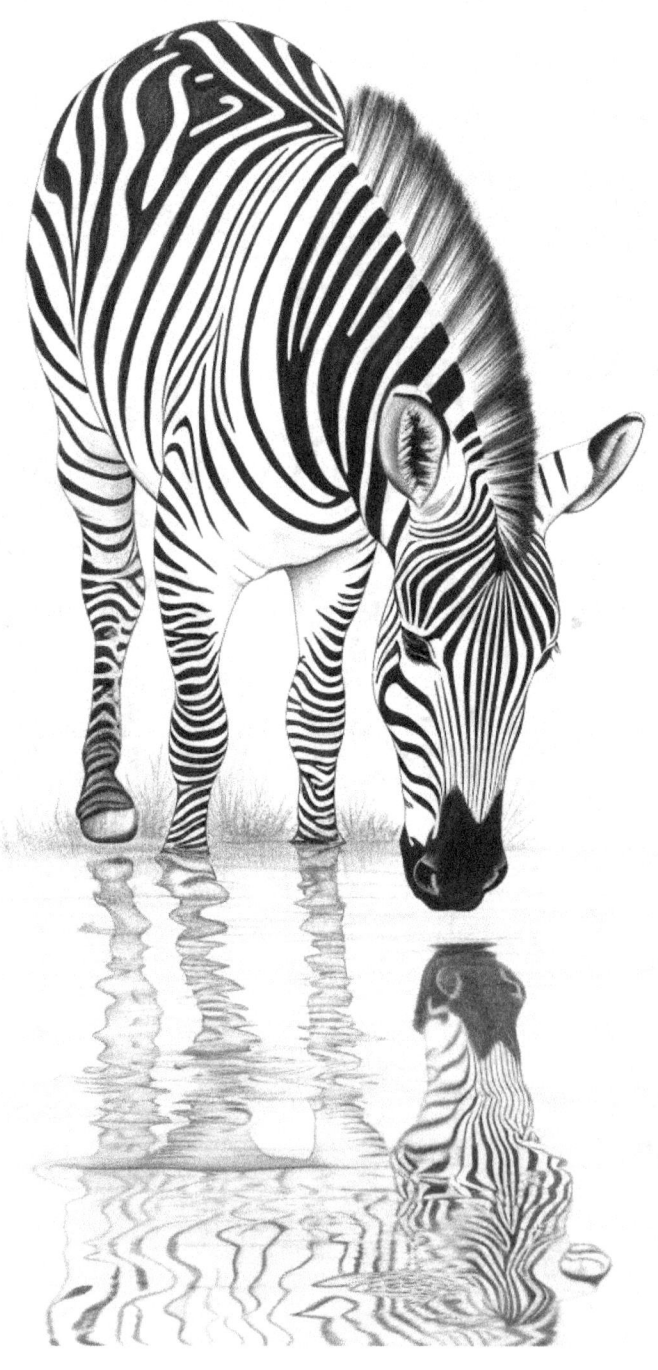

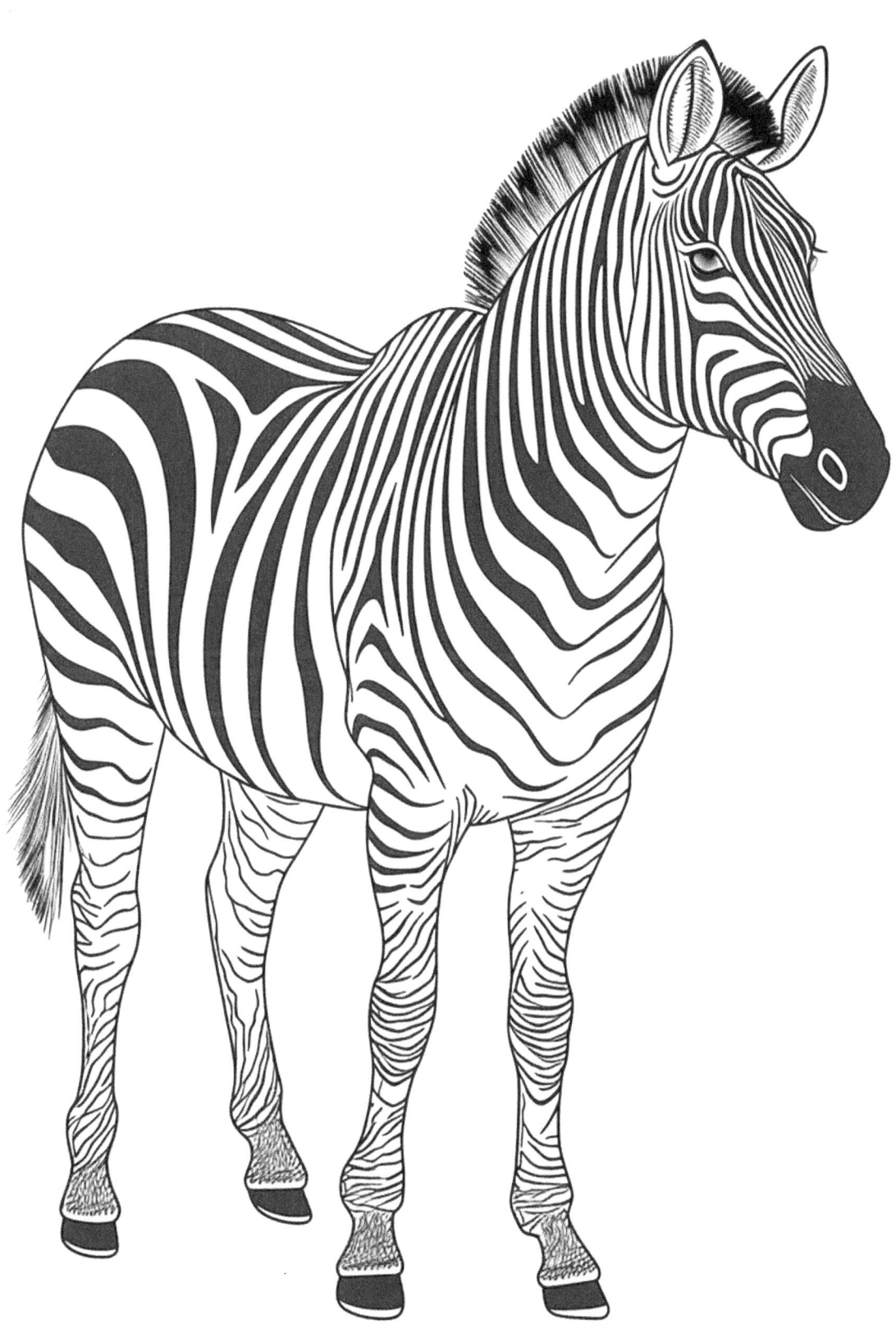

I hope you had a blast coloring these amazing animals and learning about their habitats and unique features. Remember, there are so many more incredible animals out there waiting to be discovered!

By exploring and appreciating the diversity of life on Earth, we can learn to be responsible stewards of our planet and protect these magnificent creatures for generations to come. This sounds very much out of character from who I am most of the time, but not everything we do has to be a huge movement, sometimes just a small change causes the right ripple.

Thank you for joining us on this fun and educational journey. Don't forget to share your colorful creations with your family and friends and keep on learning about the fascinating world of animals!

ABOUT THE AUTHOR

I am a father of four, and now a grandfather of two. I wanted my kids, and their kids to have something to remember dad or poppop by when I'm too old to be there.

I want them to hear my voice when they read these rhymes. It's probably going to be vastly different from the dad or poppop they grew up with, but time changes all memories.